ISBN 978-1-331-07108-2
PIBN 10141010

This book is a reproduction of an important historical work. Forgotten Books uses
state-of-the-art technology to digitally reconstruct the work, preserving the original format
whilst repairing imperfections present in the aged copy. In rare cases, an imperfection in
the original, such as a blemish or missing page, may be replicated in our edition. We do,
however, repair the vast majority of imperfections successfully; any imperfections that
remain are intentionally left to preserve the state of such historical works.

English
Français
Deutsche
Italiano
Español
Português

www.forgottenbooks.com

Mythology Photography **Fiction**
Fishing Christianity **Art** Cooking
Essays Buddhism Freemasonry
Medicine **Biology** Music **Ancient
Egypt** Evolution Carpentry Physics
Dance Geology **Mathematics** Fitness
Shakespeare **Folklore** Yoga Marketing
Confidence Immortality Biographies
Poetry **Psychology** Witchcraft
Electronics Chemistry History **Law**
Accounting **Philosophy** Anthropology
Alchemy Drama Quantum Mechanics
Atheism Sexual Health **Ancient History**
Entrepreneurship Languages Sport
Paleontology Needlework Islam
Metaphysics Investment Archaeology
Parenting Statistics Criminology
Motivational

PAROCHIALIA;

OR,

INSTRUCTIONS TO THE CLERGY.

PAROCHIALIA;

OR,

INSTRUCTIONS

TO

THE CLERGY.

BY THE

GHT REV. THOMAS WILSON, D.D.

SOMETIME LORD BISHOP OF SODOR AND MAN.

OXFORD:
JOHN HENRY PARKER.
MDCCCXL.

OXFORD:
PRINTED BY I. SHRIMPTON.

PREFACE.

—

IT has been much to be regretted, that Bishop Wilson's Manuals for the Clergy, have not been better known. His Sacra Privata, which was first compiled for his own use, and by which he in the next place designed to furnish his brethren with heads for meditation and devotion, has been known chiefly as stripped of its characteristics, and adapted to general use. And the Parochialia, which breathes the same deep earnestness, the same touching simplicity, and affectionate thoughtfulness for the direction of his Clergy in the most difficult part. of their duty, and the most minute consideration of the very least spiritual wants of every member of the flock, has rarely been printed separately.

It has been truly said of the Sacra Privata, that " those devotional exercises, or the like of them, are the groundwork of whatever name and influence he has attained in the Church of God." As no one felt more deeply, that the Ordinances of the Church, as administered in the Name of Christ, depend not on the "power and holiness" of man: so was no one more keenly alive to the necessity and influence of personal piety in the Steward of the mysteries of God. The Parochialia implies this throughout; explaining the "means of grace," and insisting on deep reverence in dispensing them, but giving as the only secret of attaining it, constancy and seriousness in private prayer and Christian practice. Thus with Bishop Wilson all is

naturalness and reality : none better exempli-
fied nor taught more truly the beautiful lesson
of Herbert, that the "Parson's library is a holy
life :"—and his "life, a visible rhetoric."

His Sacra Privata might be summed up in
the prayer of the Psalmist; "O give me the
comfort of Thy help, and stablish me with
Thy free Spirit ;—*then* shall I teach Thy ways
unto the wicked, and sinners shall be converted unto Thee."

And this work, in the same spirit, seems
to say in the most affecting manner to every
Parish Priest, "When thou art converted,
strengthen thy brethren."

The Bishop's Instructions for an Academic
Youth, and his Catechetical Instructions for
Candidates for Holy Orders, are added.

And the Forms of Excommunication and
Receiving Penitents, seem indispensable,
because the question of Church Discipline is

with him so entirely sacred and practical, its existence so often assumed, and its enforcement so interwoven with all his teaching; that neither of these works would be adequately understood without them. It forms the main subject for Meditation for Thursday in the Sacra Privata, and is a prominent feature in the Parochialia. It is enforced in his Ecclesiastical Constitutions, and Private Letters to his Clergy.—In fact, the Diocese of Sodor and Man, under his care, exhibited more perfectly than has been seen in modern times, the Church, as a whole;—and it was truly said, that if the "ancient Discipline of the Church were lost, it might be found in all its purity in the Isle of Man."

W. J. C.

Trin. Coll. Oxford,
    July 1, 1840.

CONTENTS.

PAROCHIALIA.

CONTENTS.

FORM OF EXCOMMUNICATION.

FORM OF RECEIVING PENITENTS.

PAROCHIALIA.

TO

THE CLERGY

OF

THE DIOCESE

OF

SODOR AND MAN.

Bishop's Court, March 3d, 1708.

MY DEAR BRETHREN,

I PERSUADE myself, that you will take the following advice well from me, because, besides the authority God has given me, I have always encouraged you to give me your assistance to enable me to discharge my duty.

Every return of Lent (a time when people were wont either to call themselves, or to be called, to an account) should put *us*, above all men, upon examining and judging ourselves, because we are to answer for the faith and manners of others, as well as for our own; and therefore this is a very proper season to take an account both of our flocks and of ourselves, which would make our great account less hazardous and dreadful.

Let me therefore entreat you, at this time, to do what I have obliged myself to; namely, carefully to look over your Ordination Vows. It is very commendable to do this every Ember-week; but it would be unpardonable negligence not once a year to consider what we have bound ourselves to, and taken the Sacrament upon it.

In the first place, therefore, *If we were indeed* " *moved by the Holy Ghost,*" *and* " *truly called to the Ministry of the Church,*" as we declared we were, this will appear in our conduct ever since. Let us then consider, Whether our great aim has been to promote the glory of God with which we were intrusted, and the eternal interest of the souls committed to our charge, according to the vows that are upon us? If not, for God's sake, let us put on resolutions of better obedience for the time to come.

The Holy Scriptures are the rule by which we and our people are to be judged at the last day; it is for this we solemnly promise, " *To be diligent in reading, and to instruct our people out of the same Holy Scriptures.*" They do indeed " *sufficiently contain all doctrine necessary to eternal salvation,*" (as we profess to believe,) but then they must be carefully studied, often consulted, and the Holy Spirit often applied to, for the true understanding of them; or else in vain is all our labour, and we are false to our vows.

Upon which heads it will behove us to consider, How much we have neglected this necessary study; how often we have contented ourselves with reading just so much as we were obliged to by the public Offices of the Church! How apt such as read not the Holy Scriptures are to run to other books for matter for their Sermons; by which means they have been too often led to speak of errors and vices, which did no way concern their hearers, or of things above their capacities:—and it has often happened, that they themselves have scarce been convinced of (and of course have not been heartily in love with) the truths which they have recommended to others, which is the true reason why their Sermons may have done so little good.

But when a man is sensibly affected with the value of souls, with the danger they are in, with the manner of their redemption, and the price paid for them; and is well acquainted with the New Testament, in which all this is plainly set forth; as he will never want matter for the best Sermons, so he will never want arguments sufficient to convince his hearers, his own heart being touched with the importance of the subject. Under this head, we must not forget to charge ourselves with the duty of Catechising: for, as it is one of the most necessary duties of the Ministry, so it is bound upon us by Laws, Canons, Rubrics, and Constitutions, enough to awaken the most careless among us to a more diligent discharge of this duty.

But though we should be never so diligent in these duties, if our conversation be not edifying, we shall only bring these Ordinances into contempt; and therefore, when a Priest is ordained, he promises, " *by God's help, to frame and fashion himself and family, so as to make both, as much as in him lieth, wholesome examples and patterns of the flock of Christ.*"

Under which head, it will be fit to consider, what offence we may have given, by an unwary conversation, by criminal liberties, &c. that we may beg God's pardon, and make some amends by a more strict behaviour for the future; that we may be examples to the flock, teaching them sobriety, by our strict temperance; charity, by our readiness to forgive; devotion, by our ardent zeal in the offering up their prayers to God.

They that think all their work is done, when the service of the Lord's Day is over, do not remember, that they have promised to " *use both public and private monitions, as well to the sick as to the whole, within their Cures, as need shall require, and as occasion shall be given."* Upon this head, let us look back and see, how often we have forborn to reprove open offenders, either out of fear, or from a sinful modesty, or for worldly respects:—considerations which should never come in competition with the honour of God, with which a Clergyman stands charged.

Let us consider, how few we have admonished privately; how few we have reclaimed; and how many, who are yet under the power of a sinful life, which we might have reclaimed by such admonitions!

Let us consider, how many have been in affliction of mind, body, or estate, without any benefit to their souls, for want of being made sensible of the hand, and voice, and design of God in such visitations! How many have recovered from the bed of sickness, without becoming better men, only for want of being put in mind of the fears they were under, and the thoughts they had, and the promises they made, when they were in danger!—Lastly; How many have lived and died in sin, without making their peace with God, or satisfaction and restitution to man, for want of being forewarned of the account they were to give! A negligence which we cannot reflect upon without trembling.

It will here likewise be proper to consider, how many offenders have escaped the censures of the Church through our neglect, by which they might have been humbled for their sins, and others restrained from falling into the like miscarriages. Other Churches lament the want of that discipline, which we (blessed be God!) can exercise. How great then is the sin of those, who, by laziness or partiality, would bring it into disuse.

Because a great deal depends upon the manner of our performing Divine Offices, we ought to reflect upon it, how often we read the Prayers of the Church with coldness and indevotion, and administer the Sacraments with an indifference unworthy of the holy Mysteries; by which it comes to pass, that some despise, and some abhor, the service of God! Let us detest such indevotion, and resolve upon a becoming seriousness, when we offer up the supplications of the people to God, that they, seeing our zeal, may be persuaded, that it is not for trifles we pray, nor out of custom only that we go to church.

The great secret of attaining such an affecting way is, to be constant and serious in our private devotions, which will beget in us a spirit of piety, able to influence our voice and actions.

Having thus taken an account of our own engagements, and heartily begged God's pardon for our omissions, and prescribed rules to ourselves, of acting suitably to our high calling for the future, we shall be better disposed to take an account of our flock: always remembering, that our love to Christ is to be expressed by feeding His sheep.

I have observed with satisfaction, that most people, who by their age are qualified, do come to the Lord's Supper at Easter. Now, it is much to be feared, that such as generally turn their backs upon that holy Ordinance at other times, do come at this time more out of custom, or to comply with the laws, than out of a sense of duty.

This is no way to be prevented, but by giving them a true notion of this holy Sacrament, such as shall neither encourage the profane to eat and drink their own damnation, nor discourage well-meaning people from receiving the greatest comfort and support of the Christian life.

To this end it will be highly conducive, (and I earnestly recommend it to you,) to make this the subject of a good part of your Sermons during Lent. But let them be plain and practical discourses, such as may set forth the nature, end, and benefits of the Lord's Supper. That it is to keep up the remembrance of the Sacrifice and Death of Christ, whereby alone we obtain remission of our sins, and all other benefits of His Passion. That it is a mark of our being members of Christ's Church, a token of our being in covenant with God. That a sinner has nothing but this to plead for pardon, when the devil or his conscience accuse him before God. That we ought to receive as often as conveniently we can, that, as Peter Damien expresses himself, "*the old serpent, seeing the Blood of the Lamb upon our lips, may tremble to approach us.*" That Jesus Christ presents before God in Heaven His death and merits, for all such as duly remember them on earth.

Let them know, that a Christian life is the best preparation; that God respects sincerity of heart above all things; which consists in doing what God has commanded us, to the best of our knowledge and power.

Let them know the danger of unworthy receiving, without full purposes of amendment of life. And, that they may know wherein they have offended, and that they may have no cloak for their sin, it would be very convenient, some Sunday before Easter, to read to them some heads of self-examination, (leaving out such sins and duties in which none of them are concerned,) such as you will find at the latter end of the Whole Duty of Man, and in many other books of devotion.

But to make your Sermons more effectual, (and I desire it and require it of you,) that you take an account of the state and condition of your particular flocks during the approaching season, and visit and deal in private with those upon whom your Sermons have probably had no influence.

Let them know, that the Church obliges you to deny them the blessed Sacrament, which is the means of salvation, until you can be satisfied of their reformation.

Let such as live in malice, envy, or in any other grievous crime, and yet come to the holy Table as if they were in a state of salvation; let them be told, that they provoke God to plague them with His judgments.

Admonish such as are litigious, and vex their neighbours without cause, that this is contrary to the spirit and rules of Christianity; that this holy Sacrament either finds or makes all Communicants of one heart and mind, or mightily increases their guilt that are not made so.

Tell such as are wont, before that solemn

season of receiving, to forbear drinking and their other vices,—that fast and pray for a few days;—tell them plainly, that none of these exercises are acceptable to God, which are not attended with amendment of life.

Rebuke severely such as despise and profane the Lord's Day; make them sensible, that a curse must be upon that family, out of which none goes to church to obtain a blessing upon those that stay at home.

Tell such as have submitted to Church censures, and are not become better men, how abominable that hypocrisy is, that made them utter the most solemn promises, which they never meant to keep.

By this method, you will answer the ends of that Rubric before the Communion, which requires all persons that design to receive, to " *signify their names to the Curate at least some time the day before;*" an order which, if observed, would give us rare opportunities of admonishing offenders, who yet do not think themselves in danger.

Lastly; in making this visitation, you will see what children are uncatechised, what families have no face of religion in them, &c.

But for God's sake remember, that if all this be not done in the spirit of meekness, with prudence and sweetness, you will never attain the end proposed by such a visitation of your parish.

Do but consider, with what goodness our blessed Master treated sinners, and you will bear much in order to reduce them. At the same time, fear not the face of any man, while you are engaged in the cause of God, and in the way of your duty. He will either defend you, or reward your sufferings, and can when He pleases terrify gainsayers.

It is true, all this is not to be done without trouble; but then consider, what grief, and weariness, and contempt, our Master underwent, in turning sinners from the power of Satan unto God: and as He saw the travail of His soul, so shall we reap great benefit by it even in this world.

We shall have great satisfaction in seeing

our churches thronged with Communicants, who come out of a sense of duty more than out of a blind obedience. We shall gain a wonderful authority amongst our people. Such as have any spark of grace will love and respect you for your friendly admonition. Such as have none will however reverence you, and stand in awe of you. And they that pay you tithes, will by this be convinced, that it is not for doing nothing that you receive them, since your calling obliges you to continual labour and thoughts of heart.

That you may do all this with a spirit of piety worthy of the Priesthood, you have two excellent books in your hands, "The Pastoral Care," and "The Country Parson," which I hope I need not enjoin you to read over at this time.

I considered, that the best men have sometimes need of being stirred up, that they may not lose a spirit of piety which is but too apt to languish. This is all the apology I shall make for this address to you at this time.

Now, that both you and I may give a comfortable account of our office and charge, as it is the design of this *Letter*, so it shall be my hearty prayer to God.

I am,

Your affectionate Brother,

THOMAS SODOR AND MAN.

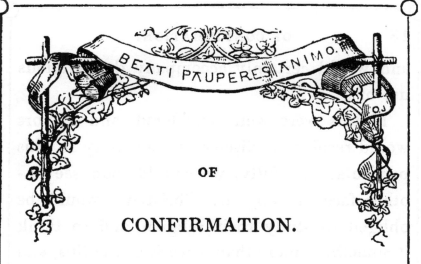

OF

CONFIRMATION.

OF ANSWERING THE ENDS OF THIS APOSTOLICAL INSTITUTION.

THERE is no question to be made of it, but that most of that ignorance, impiety, profaneness, want of charity, of union, and order, which we complain of, is owing to the neglect or abuse of this one Ordinance; which being appointed by the Apostles, and practised even when Baptism was administered to people of full age[a], it is no wonder that God punishes the contempt of it, by withholding His Holy Spirit, and those graces which are necessary,

[a] Acts viii. 17.

and would certainly accompany the religious use of it.

If this were well considered, and Pastors would resolve to discharge their duty in this particular faithfully, we should soon see another face of religion: Christians would be obliged to study their religion, and to think it something more than a work of the lips, and of the memory, or the mere custom of the place where they live. And being made sensible of their danger, (being liable to *sin*, to *death*, and to *damnation*,) this would make them *serious*, and *thoughtful*, and *inquisitive*, after the manner of their redemption, and the means of salvation; and their consciences being awakened and informed, sin would become more uneasy to them, and virtue more acceptable. In short, by this means, people would know their duty, the Sacraments would be kept from being profaned, and Pastors would be respected and obeyed, as being very truly the fathers of their flock.

And certainly no greater injury can be done to religion, than to suffer young people to come to Confirmation, before they know the reason of this Service, and have been well instructed in the principles and duties of Christianity:—This being the very time of seasoning their minds with sound knowledge, of fortifying their wills with sober resolutions, and of engaging them to piety, before sin has got the possession of their affections; this being also the time of qualifying them to receive benefit by all our future labours, and of arming them against apostasy, heresy, schism, and all other vices, to which we are subject in this state of trial.

In short, I do not know how a Clergyman could possibly spend one month better, than by leading young people, as it were by the hand, into the design of Christianity, by some such easy method as this following: which, if deliberately proposed to every single person in the hearing of all the rest, (who should be obliged to be every day present,) and familiarly explained, not the most ignorant, (supposing he had learned, as he ought, the Church Catechism,) but would be able to give a reason of the hope that is in him; and his faith, being thus built upon a solid and sure foundation, would, by the grace of God now imparted to him in a greater measure, stand all future trials and temptations.

THE METHOD OF DEALING WITH YOUNG CHRIS-
TIANS, IN ORDER TO FIT THEM FOR CON-
FIRMATION.

I DO not ask you, whether you believe in God: you cannot open your eyes but you must, by the world that you see, acknowledge the God that made it, and does still preserve it; that He is infinite in power, in wisdom, and in goodness; that in Him we live, and move, and have our being; that He is therefore worthy of all the love and service that we can possibly pay Him.

How then do you think it comes to pass, that so many, who profess to know God, do yet in works deny Him[b]? Why; this shews plainly, that man is fallen from that good estate in which God created him. He knows that he ought to live righteously, as in the sight of an holy and just God; that he should

[b] Tit. i. 16.

be afraid of doing any thing to offend so powerful a Being; that he should love, and strive to please Him, upon whose goodness he depends; and that he should obey all His laws. And yet he cannot prevail with himself to do what he is persuaded he ought to do.

This may convince you, that man's nature has been sadly corrupted some way or other; we having, in every one of us, the seeds of all manner of wickedness, which, if not kept under, will certainly grow up and be our ruin.

Now, the Holy Scriptures tell you how this came to pass; namely, that our first parents being created perfect, (that is, able to know and obey any law that God should give them,) God gave them the law of nature and right reason to live by, and required of them a perfect obedience, with this assurance, that they should never die, if they did not transgress one particular command, of not eating the forbidden fruit; which command was given them both to try their obedience, and to keep their appetites in subjection.

Now, they did transgress this command, and thereby became subject to sin, to death, the reward of sin, and to the wrath of God: for God withdrew the supernatural powers and graces which He had given them, so that now, though they knew what was fit to be done, yet had they no longer power to perform it; which would certainly have driven them to despair, but that God was pleased immediately to comfort them with this promise; That a time was coming, when He would send One to redeem them and their posterity from this miserable bondage; and that He would then receive them again into favour, upon reasonable conditions.

In the mean time, Adam begat a race of children after his own likeness[c]; that is, with such a corrupt nature as his own was now become; and his posterity grew every day more and more wicked, till at last God destroyed the whole world (except eight persons) by a flood.

But this did not destroy the seeds of sin which was in them; for by these eight persons

[c] Gen. v. 3.

the world was peopled with a race of men, who in a short time did quite forget and forsake God; and for the most part became the subjects of the devil, and were led captives by him at his will.

At last, God remembered His promise, and, resolving to mend that disorder which sin had caused in the world, He sent His Son to take our nature upon Him, and to give mankind assurance, that God would be reconciled to them upon very merciful conditions; namely, if they would renounce the devil, who first tempted man to sin, and accept of such laws and rules as were necessary to change their nature, which was now become prone to evil continually.

Now, to assure them that Jesus Christ came with this message from God, He did such miracles as none but God could do; and to convince us how much He loved us, and what a sad thing sin is, (which nothing but His death could atone for,) He gave His life a ransom for us; the punishment due to *us* being laid on *Him*.

And God, to let us know that He was well-pleased with what His Son had *done*, and *taught*, and *suffered*, raised Him to life after He had been crucified, and received Him up into Heaven, and gave Him all power in Heaven and in earth, and sent down the Holy Ghost, with mighty power, to set up His Kingdom, which is His Church, among men; to destroy the kingdom of Satan, who hitherto had ruled without control; and to free mankind from the tyranny and slavery of sin.

In order to this, the Holy Ghost appointed certain persons, (who are called Christ's Ministers,) and gave them power to receive into His Church, all such as would promise to obey His laws.

Your parents therefore took care, (as the Jews did by their children,) to consecrate you to God and Christ, as soon as you were born. And this they did by Baptism, (as Jesus Christ had commanded,) by which holy ceremony you were dedicated to *God*, Who *made* you: to *Jesus Christ*, Who *redeemed* you; and to the *Holy Ghost*, Who *sanctifieth* all God's chosen servants.

Thus you were translated (or taken) out of the kingdom of darkness, into the kingdom, protection, and government of Jesus Christ[d]: and being thus received into Christ's Church, you became a child of God, and an heir of the Kingdom of Heaven.

But then you are to consider, that before you were admitted to this favour, your sureties promised for you, that when you should come to age, you should in your own person, and with your own free consent, renounce the devil and all his works, the world and all its wicked customs, and the flesh with all its sinful lusts: that you should believe in God, that is, receive the Gospel as a rule of faith; and obediently keep God's commandments.

You are now therefore called upon to do this before God, Who knows all the secrets of your hearts; before God's Minister, who will charge you very solemnly to be sincere: and before the congregation, who will be

[d] Col. i. 13.

witnesses against you, if you shall break your vows.

I must tell you farther, that to root or keep out evil habits, and to get habits of virtue, and to live as becomes a Christian, is not so easily done as promised.

You will be obliged to take pains, to watch and pray, and deny yourself, and even lay down your life, rather than deny your profession, or dissemble it.

But then you will not think this too much, when you consider, that it is for your life, and that it is to escape eternal death.

For Jesus Christ has made known to us, That this life is a state of trial, and only a passage to another life, where God will take an account, how all men have behaved themselves here, and appoint them a portion suitable to what they have done in the body, whether good or bad: *When they that have done good shall go into life everlasting: and they that have done evil, into everlasting misery.*

Now, that you may not despair of going through the work of your salvation, and getting the victory over all your enemies, Jesus Christ hath sent down His Holy Spirit to be communicated, by the " laying on of hands[e]," to all such as are disposed to receive Him ; by which Almighty Spirit, all your enemies shall be subdued, all your lusts mortified, your corruptions rooted out, and your soul purified; so that when you die, you will be fit to be carried to the quiet and happy regions of Paradise, where the souls of the faithful enjoy perpetual rest and happiness.

Every Christian, who is preparing himself for Confirmation, ought to have this or some such short account of the method of Divine grace read to him distinctly, (and explained where there is need,) once every day for one month, at least, before that holy Ordinance; that he may remember it as long as he lives, and be able to give a reason of the hope that is in him.

[e] Acts. viii. 17. Heb. vi. 2.

But, forasmuch as he is to renew his vows before God, Who will be provoked with the hypocrisy and impiety of those who promise what they do not understand, or what they do not think of performing, a good Pastor will not fail to ask every person, in the presence of the rest, (that by hearing them often, they may be better able to remember them,) some such questions as these following:—

OF RENOUNCING THE DEVIL, &c.

ARE you convinced, that you ought to love God, as He is the Author of all good, and *upon Whom you depend for life, and breath, and all things?*

Why then consider, that you cannot possibly love God, unless you renounce the love of every thing that may displease Him.

Do you know that all sin is displeasing to God, as being the transgression of His law[f]?

Do you therefore renounce all sin, and every thing that would draw you from God?

Do you renounce the *devil*, the great enemy of God and man; all his *works*, such as pride, malice, revenge, and lying; and wicked men, which are his agents?

Do you know that this is not the world you were made for; that it is only a passage to another?

[f] 1 John iii. 4.

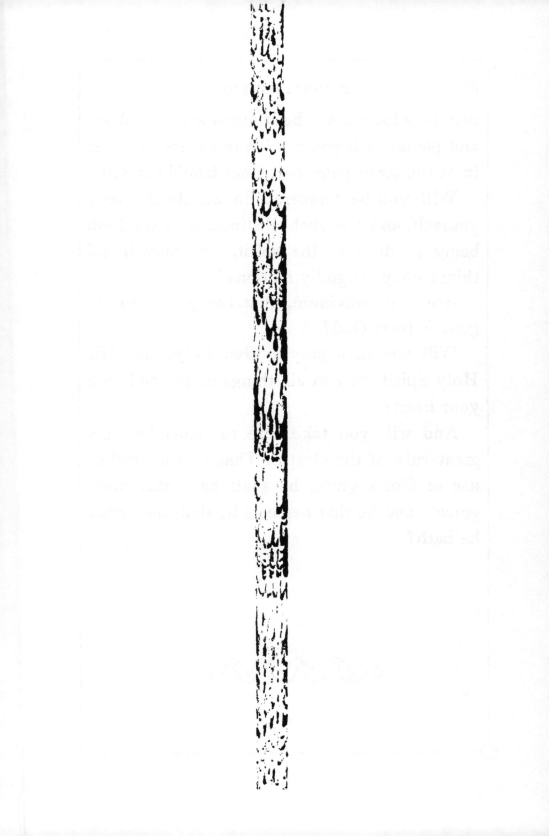

... and peace will you ...

in ... will you ...

Will you be faithful to ...

yourself, and ... faithful ... such

being a child of the Church, ... make ...

things anew in Holy Spirit ...

... from God?

Will you be a true and faithful ... the

Holy Spirit may in all things be ... in

your heart?

And will you take up to serve the

great rule of the Church? That the ordi-

use of God's grace, ... shall be ... steadfast

grace ... to what need not be, shall ever

be holy?

blessings too great to be attained without labour and pains; will you resolve in earnest to enter in at the strait gate, cost what trouble it will?

Will you be temperate in all things, deny yourself, and use such abstinence, as the flesh being subdued to the spirit, you may in all things obey all godly motions?

Are you convinced, that the power to do good is from God?

Will you then pray to God daily, that His Holy Spirit may in all things direct and rule your heart?

And will you take care to remember this great rule of the Gospel, That he that makes use of God's grace, he shall have still more grace; and he that neglects it, shall lose what he hath?

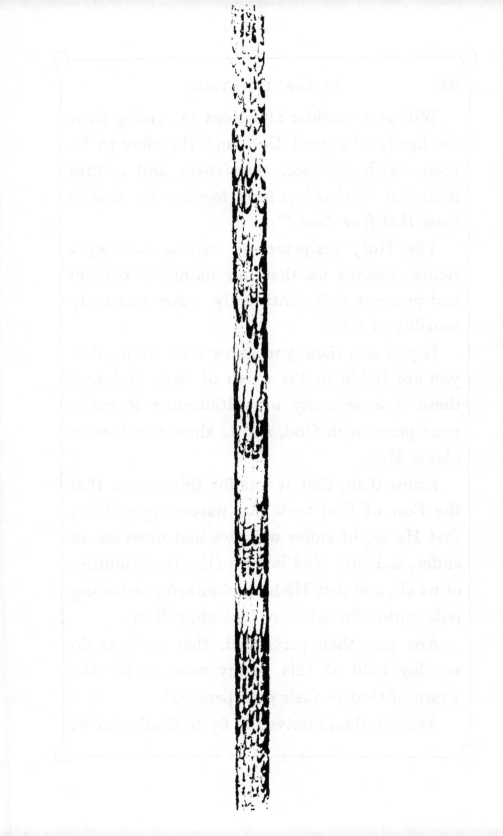

Will you consider afflictions as coming from the hands of a good God, and therefore to be borne with *patience, submission,* and a firm faith *that " all things work together for good to those that fear God ?"*

The Holy Scripture, as well as sad experience, assures us, that our nature is corrupt and prone to evil continually. Are you truly sensible of this?

If you are, then you know for certain, that you are liable to the wrath of God, and that there is a necessity of a Redeemer to make your peace with God, and to shew you how to please Him.

Know then, that it was for this reason that the Son of God took our nature upon Him, that He might suffer what we had deserved to suffer, and that God laid on Him the iniquities of us all, and that He hath obtained everlasting redemption for all them that obey Him.

Are you then persuaded, that such as do not lay hold of this mercy must suffer the wrath of God in their own persons?

Are you then resolved to fly to God's mercy,

for Christ's sake, to obey His laws, and follow His example?

Will you always endeavour to do what you believe Christ would do, if He were in your place and circumstances?

Will you set before your eyes His *sufferings*, His *humility*, His *patience*, His *charity*, and His *submission to the will of God*, in order to *direct*, to *support*, and *comfort* you in all your troubles?

And remember that Jesus Christ is now in Heaven, in His human nature, evermore interceding for all that go to God by Him.

Do you firmly believe all that God hath made known to us by His Son?

Do you believe that we must all appear before the Judgment-seat of Christ, by Whose righteous sentence, *they that have done good shall go into life everlasting, and they that have done evil into everlasting misery?*

Will you then live like one that believes all this; being careful of all your thoughts, words, and actions, which must then be judged?

Do you know that in Baptism we are dedicated to the Holy Ghost, because it is He who must sanctify our nature, and fit us by His graces for Heaven?

Will you then pray earnestly to God, and especially at this time, to give you this blessing, since He Himself hath promised " *to give the Holy Spirit to them that ask Him ?*"

Will you order your life according to that Word which He inspired, and take care not to grieve Him by continuing in any known sin?

And since you are taught and governed by a Bishop and Pastors commissioned by the Holy Ghost[g]; will you therefore live in obedience to them, to whom Jesus Christ made this promise[h], "*Lo, I am with you always, even unto the end of the world ?*"

Will you treat all Christian people with love and charity, as being members of that Body, of which Jesus Christ is the Head?

Will you hope for forgiveness of sins for Christ's sake only, and believe that the goodness of God ought to lead you to repentance?

[g] Acts xx. 28.   [h] Matt. xxviii. 20.

Do you believe, that there will be a resurrection both of the just and unjust?

Do you faithfully believe, that after this life there will be a state of endless happiness or endless misery?

Remember then, that *a saving faith purifieth the heart;* and that a good faith must be known by its fruits, as one tree is known from another.

OF OBEDIENCE TO GOD'S COMMANDS, &c.

ARE you persuaded, that the design of all true religion is to make men holy that they may be happy?

Do you think that man is able to find out a way to please God, and to govern himself by his own reason?

So far from it, that when God left men to themselves, (as He did the heathens,) they chose the most foolish and abominable ways of serving their gods, and fell into wickednesses scarce fit to be named[i].

Will you then make the Law of God the rule of your life?

Will you be careful not to love or fear any thing more than God; for that would be your idol?

[i] Romans i.

Will you worship God with reverence; that is, upon your knees, when you ask His pardon or blessing; standing up when you praise Him; and hearing His word with attention?

Will you honour God's Name, so as not to use it but with seriousness?

Will you abhor all manner of oaths, except when you are called before a Magistrate; and will you then speak the truth, as you hope the Lord will hold you guiltless?

Will you remember to keep holy the *Lord's* Day, as that which sanctifies the whole week?

Will you honour your parents, and be subject to the higher powers, obeying all their lawful commands?

Will you reverence your Pastors, and take in good part all their godly admonitions?

Will you be careful not to hurt, or wish any man's death, not be glad at misfortunes, or grieve men without cause?

Will you be gentle and easy to be entreated, that God for Christ's sake may be so towards you?

Will you remember that whoredom and sins of impurity will certainly keep men out of Heaven?

Do you believe that restitution is a necessary duty, (where it can be made,) without which there is no forgiveness?

If you believe this, you will never wrong any body by force, fraud, or by colour of law; you will pay all your just debts, and never take advantage of any man's necessity.

Will you remember that the God of truth hateth lying,—that the devil is the father of lies,—and that liars, slanderers, and backbiters, are to have their portion in the lake that burneth with fire and brimstone[k]?

Will you endeavour to be content with your own condition, neither envying that of others, nor bettering your own by unjust ways?

Will you in all your actions have an eye to God; and say to yourself, I do *this*, or forbear *that, because God hath commanded me?*

[k] Rev. xxi. 8.

Will you remember this good rule, never to undertake any thing which you dare not pray God to prosper?

Are you convinced, that all power to do good is from God; and that without His grace, you cannot keep His commandments?

Will you then pray to God daily, that His Holy Spirit may in all things direct and rule your heart?

May the gracious God enable you to do what you have now resolved upon!

You are now going to profess yourself a member of the Church of Christ.

Will you then endeavour to become a worthy member of that Society?

Will you make the Gospel of Christ your rule to walk by; and obey them that are over you in the Lord?

Will you promise, by the grace of God, to continue in the unity of this Church, of which you are now going to be made a complete member?

If you should be so unhappy as hereafter to fall into any scandalous sin, will you patiently submit to be reformed by godly discipline?

Will you be very careful not to let wicked and profane people laugh you out of these holy purposes and resolutions, remembering the words of Jesus Christ: *He that denieth Me, him will God deny?*

———

If this short method were conscientiously observed by every Curate of souls, for thirty or forty days before every Confirmation, and two or three hours every day spent in reading deliberately the short account of religion, and in asking every particular person the questions, in the hearing of all the rest, (which, according to our constitution, ought not to be above thirty or forty at one time,) I will venture to say, that the remembrance *of this duty*, would be of more comfort to a Pastor on his death-bed, than *of all the rest of his labours.*

A PRAYER THAT MAY BE USED EVERY DAY DURING THE TIME OF INSTRUCTION.

O LORD, graciously behold these Thy servants, who, according to the appointments of Thy Church, are going to dedicate themselves to Thee, and to Thy service.

Possess their hearts with such a lively sense of Thy great mercy, in bringing them from the power of Satan unto God;—in giving them an early right to Thy covenant, and an early knowledge of their duty; that, with the full consent of their wills, they may devote themselves to Thee; that so they may receive the fulness of Thy grace, and be able to withstand the temptations of the *devil*, the *world*, and the *flesh*.

Continue them, O Lord, in the unity of Thy Church, and grant that they may improve all the means of grace vouchsafed them in this Church of which they are members.

○──────────────────────────○

Preserve in their minds a constant remembrance of that love, which they are going to renew before Thee and Thy Church.

That knowing they are the servants of the living God, they may walk as in Thy sight, avoid all such things as are contrary to their profession, and follow all such as are agreeable to the same.

O Lord, Who hast made them Thy children by adoption, bring them in Thy good time to Thine everlasting Kingdom, through Jesus Christ our Lord. *Amen.*

OF THE

LORD'S SUPPER.

THE METHOD OF INSTRUCTING SUCH AS HAVE BEEN CONFIRMED, IN ORDER TO PREPARE THEM FOR THIS HOLY ORDINANCE.

I<small>F</small> Christians do frequently turn their backs upon this Sacrament, and are not concerned to have it often administered, or seem little affected when they do partake of it, one may certainly conclude, *they never truly understood the meaning of it.*

This might surely, in some measure, be prevented, if due pains were taken to give young people a distinct knowledge of *this most important duty* ; and of the manner of preparing themselves for it, before they should be admitted *the first time* to the Sacrament; for want of which, very many continue in a gross ignorance, both of the meaning and benefits of this Ordinance all their days.

A good Pastor, therefore, will not suffer any one to come to the Holy Communion until he has taken pains to examine and to inform him very particularly concerning the *meaning* of this Ordinance, and the *ends* for which it was appointed;—what this Sacrament *obliges* Christians to, and the benefits they may expect from it;—with what *dispositions* a Christian should come to it, and the great sin of despising it.

The young Christian should, for instance, be put in mind, that as there were in the Jewish, so there are in the Christian Church, "two Sacraments."

That the Sacrament of *Baptism* was ordained by Christ for admitting us into His Church upon certain conditions, which such as are baptized in their infancy are to perform when they come to age.

And the *Holy Supper* He ordained, that

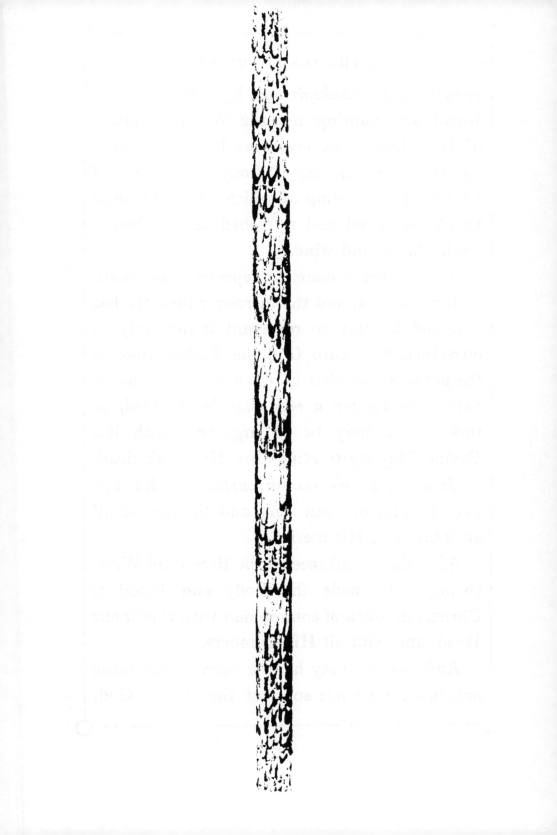

prayer and *thanksgiving*, by breaking the Bread and pouring out the Wine, obtaineth of God that these creatures become, after a spiritual manner, the " Body and Blood of Christ," by receiving of which our souls shall be strengthened and refreshed as our bodies are by bread and wine.

For all this is done, to represent the death of Jesus Christ, and the mercies which He has obtained for us; to represent it not only to ourselves, but unto God the Father, that *as the prayers and alms of Cornelius are said to have gone up for a memorial before God*, so this service may be an argument with His Divine Majesty to remember His Son's death in *Heaven*, as we do on *earth*, and for His sake to blot out our sins, and to give us all an interest in His merits.

After this we all receive the Bread and Wine, (being thus made the Body and Blood of Christ,) in token of communion with Christ our Head, and with all His members.

And that we may have a more lively sense imprinted upon our souls of the *love* of God,

cern to Christians, it is no wonder, that the Church, directed by St. Paul, very seriously exhorts all Christians to examine and to prepare themselves for this holy Ordinance; for if a Christian should presume to come to the Lord's Table, without knowing what he is going to do, without *repentance*, without *purposes of leading a Christian life*, without *faith* in God's mercy through Christ, without *a thankful heart*, and without *charity*, he will receive a *curse* instead of a *blessing*.

Because many Christians, therefore, especially the younger sort, may not know upon what heads, and after what manner, they ought to examine themselves, or lest they should do it by halves, or perhaps not at all, a faithful Pastor will shew them the way, by examining them himself, after this or some such like plain method.

CONCERNING THEIR REPENTANCE.

Do you know that God will not accept of the service of such as live in the practice of any known sin?

Let me therefore advise you, as you love your soul, to consider seriously, Whether you are subject to any evil habit, either of *lying*, or *swearing*, or *drinking*; or of any sin of *uncleanness*; or of an *idle life*, which will lead to these? And if you find you are, your duty is to judge yourself, to beg God's pardon, and to amend your life.

Will you do this, and in *obedience to God*, because He requires it?

Will you promise sincerely to avoid all occasions of sin, especially of such sins as you have been most apt to fall into?

If through weakness or temptation you commit any sin, will you forthwith confess your fault to God, ask His pardon, and be more careful for the time to come?

Will you endeavour to live in the fear of God, always remembering, that a good life is the best preparation for this Sacrament?

Will you constantly pray for God's grace and assistance, without which all your good purposes will come to nothing?

Will you strive to keep your conscience tender and awake, that you may know when you sin, and that your heart may not be hardened, which is the greatest judgment?

Lastly; Will you be careful to keep a watch over yourself, that you may not fall into the sins you have repented of?

And will you often examine into the state of your soul, especially before you go to the Lord's Table, that you may see whether you grow in grace, and get the mastery over your corruptions? For if you do so, you are certainly under the government of God's Holy Spirit.

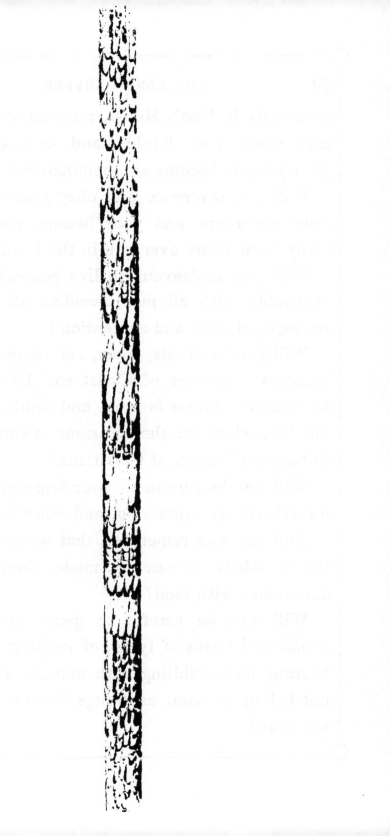

reverently in God's House, not sitting at your ease when you should stand or kneel, lest your prayers become an abomination?

Will you reverence and obey your parents, your governors, and your betters, and especially such as are over you in the Lord?

Will you endeavour to live peaceably and charitably with all men, avoiding all malice, revenge, ill-will, and contention?

Will you be chaste, sober, and temperate, as becomes a member of Christ and His family, avoiding all excess in meat and drink, and an idle life, which are the occasions of sins not fit to be named amongst Christians?

Will you be true in all your dealings, avoiding all wrong, oppression, and extortion?

And will you remember, that without restitution, where it can be made, there is no acceptance with God?

Will you be careful to speak the truth, avoiding the sins of lying, of perjury, of tale-bearing, and meddling with matters which do not belong to you, as things hateful to God and man?

Will you be content with your lot, whatever it be; neither coveting that which is another's, nor envying His prosperity, nor being glad at His calamities?

Lastly; Will you do these things out of the love and reverence you bear to God, Whose laws they are?

And will you seriously beg of Him to write all these laws in your hearts, and to incline and enable you to keep them?

HOW A CHRISTIAN SHOULD EXAMINE, WHETHER
    HE HATH A LIVELY FAITH IN GOD'S MERCY
    THROUGH CHRIST.

As the blood of the Paschal lamb sprinkled
upon their doors, was that which saved the
Israelites from death; so the Blood of Jesus
Christ is that which saves all Christians that
partake of it.

Do you stedfastly believe this?

Do you trust in Jesus Christ, and in what
He has done and suffered for you, and in Him
only, for pardon and salvation?

Do you firmly believe that Jesus Christ is
now in Heaven interceding with God, by virtue
of His death, for all such as on earth do religiously keep up the remembrance of that His
death until His coming again?

Your faith being built upon the promises of
God in Jesus Christ, and all His promises

being on condition that we live as becomes Christians; will you seriously purpose to do so?

And will you remember, not to presume on God's mercy, or expect that He will communicate His graces, while you continue under the power of a sinful life?

HOW A CHRISTIAN MAY KNOW WHETHER HE HAS A THANKFUL REMEMBRANCE OF CHRIST'S DEATH.

Do you desire to have a thankful remembrance of Christ's death?

Why then, consider what he has done for you and for all mankind, to recover us from a state of sin and misery.

We were all enemies to God by wicked works. Jesus Christ undertook to restore us again to God's favour. God therefore "*laid on Him the iniquities of us all*[1];" for the sake of His death God was pleased to overlook the untowardliness of our nature, to forgive us our sins, to look upon us as His children, to give us all the grace and assistance which we shall want; and, if we behave ourselves like His children in this state of trial, He will for

[1] Isai. liii. 6.

Christ's sake make us happy to all eternity when we die.

You see what reason we have to remember His death with thankful hearts.

Will you therefore keep these things in your heart, and shew your thankfulness for the same, by living like one who has been redeemed from death and from damnation?

And will you be sure to remember this: That Jesus Christ did indeed die to redeem us from death and hell? But then He must first redeem us from this present evil world, from our vain conversation, and from all iniquity; that is, He must make us holy, that we may be happy, for "*without holiness no man can see the Lord*m."

m Heb. xii. 14.

HOW A CHRISTIAN MAY EXAMINE AND KNOW
WHETHER HE IS IN CHARITY WITH ALL
MEN.

OUR LORD JESUS CHRIST having by His
death restored all mankind to the favour of
God, He only expects this of us: That we
should love one another as He loved us.

To this end, He hath appointed, that in
this Sacrament we should all, as members of
one family of which He is the Master, as
members of one body of which He is the
·Head,—that we should eat of one Bread in remembrance of His death, and in token of that
strict union which there ought to be amongst
all Christians.

Will you then walk in love as Christ hath
loved us, and given Himself for us?

Will you consider whether you have given
any just occasion of offence, or injured any

body, so as that you ought to ask their pardon, and make them restitution?

And that no worldly shame may hinder you from doing so, you shall hear the very direction of Christ Himself:—"*If thou bring thy gift to the Altar, and there rememberest that thy brother hath ought against thee; leave there thy gift before the Altar, and go thy way; first be reconciled to thy brother, and then come and offer thy gift*[n]."

Will you therefore desire forgiveness of all such as you have offended?

And do you forgive all that have offended you?

Can you heartily pray for every body; and will you do so?

Will you (as the Apostle directs,) love, not in word only, but in deed and in truth, that is, doing good, as well as giving good words?

You will see Jesus Christ every day in some of His members; some naked, some hungry, some in affliction, some wanting comfort, others

[n] Matt. v. 23, 24.

instruction: Will you, for His sake, be kind to them, according to their wants, and your power to help them?

After this a good Pastor will let the young Christian see the benefits of receiving as often as he has opportunity, and the great sin of turning his back upon this Ordinance.

He will, for instance, put him in mind, That all Christians being obliged to examine themselves before they go to this Sacrament; this will keep them from falling into a state of sin and security.

That if we find we grow in grace, we shall have the greatest comfort; and if we have not got ground of our corruptions, this will make us more careful.

That our faith will hereby be strengthened, when we call to remembrance what Jesus Christ hath done for us, and that His love and His power are still the same if we strive to deserve His favour.

Lastly; that by duly partaking of this holy Ordinance, we shall come to such a state, that it will be uneasy to us to offend God, and the very pleasure of our souls to obey His laws.

On the other hand, if a Christian turns his back upon this Sacrament, (without good cause,) he transgresses an express command: "*Do this in remembrance of Me.*" He shuts himself out of Christ's family; he lives without hopes, and without promises.

If therefore, he ask how often he should receive this Sacrament, he ought to have an answer in the words of an ancient writer: "*Receive it as often as you can, that the old serpent, seeing the blood of the true Paschal Lamb upon your lips, may tremble to approach you.*"

And if to these instructions, a Pastor exhort the young Christian to be very careful not to separate from the Church, in unity with which he may expect the Holy Spirit, and all other benefits of Christ's Passion:—and if He likewise require Him, at all times hereafter, before

He designs to communicate, to give His Pastor an account of it, (in obedience to the orders of the Church,) that he may receive further advice as there shall be occasion, he will have done a work worthy of a good Pastor, and will undoubtedly receive a good reward for so doing.

CONCERNING

FAMILY PRAYER.

THE very learned and pious Bishop Pearson, took occasion very often and publicly to bless God, that he was born and bred in a family in which God was worshipped daily. And certainly, it is a duty which entails very many blessings on posterity; for which reason, a Pastor should labour with all his might to introduce it into every family under his charge; at least, he should give neither himself nor his people any rest, till he has done all that lies in his power to effect so good a work; which if he does not do, this very intimation will one day rise up in judgment against him.

And, in truth, this duty is so reasonable and

advantageous, that a man, who will but set about it in good earnest, will find people less backward than at first he would imagine.

To acknowledge God to be the giver of all good gifts;—to put a man's *self*, his *wife*, his *children*, his *servants*, and all that belongs to him under God's protection;—to ask from Him, as from a Father, whatever we want,—and to thank Him for the favours we have received. These are duties which the reason of mankind closes with as soon as they are fairly proposed.

And then the advantages of family worship will be evident to the meanest capacities.

First. To begin and end the day with God, will be the likeliest way to make *servants* faithful, *children* dutiful, *wives* obedient, and *husbands* sober, loving, and careful; every one acting as in the sight of God.

Secondly. This will be a mighty check upon every one of the family, and will be a means of preventing much wickedness; at least, people will sin with remorse, (which is much better than with a seared conscience,) when every one knows he must go upon his knees before he sleeps.

Thirdly. This is the way to entail piety upon the generations to come. When children and servants, coming to have families of their own, cannot be easy till they fall into the same pious method which they have been long used to. " *Train up a child in the way he should go, and when he is old he will not depart from it* [m] ;" nor perhaps his children after him for many generations.

But if there are persons upon whom these motives make no impressions, let them know the evil consequences of neglecting this duty :—

" *That the curse of the Lord is in the house of the wicked* [n]."

" *Pour out Thine indignation,*" saith the Prophet [o], (that is, God will do so,) " *upon the families that call not upon His Name.*"

Add to this, that *ignorance, profaneness,* and a *curse,* must of necessity be in that family where God is not owned; where, as one

[m] Prov. xxii. 6.   [n] Prov. iii. 33.
[o] Jer. x. 25.

observes, not a creature but is taken care of,
not a swine but shall be served twice a day,
and God only is forgotten.—I say, he must be
worse than a heathen, whom these considerations do not influence.

I know of no reason that can be offered,
why every family in this Diocese might not be
brought to observe this duty, except this one:
that very many cannot read, and are too old to
learn the prayers provided for them; (though
it would be well if all that can read did conscientiously discharge this duty!) Now, where
this is indeed the case, I make no question, but
that with half an hour's patience and pains,
a Pastor might bring the most ignorant person
to observe this following method of orderly
devotion:

First. Let him speak to his family, and say,
Let us confess our sins to God, saying,

" *Remember not, Lord, our offences, nor the
offences of our forefathers ; neither take Thou
vengeance of our sins : spare us, good Lord,
spare Thy people whom Thou hast redeemed*

with Thy most precious Blood, and be not angry with us for ever."

Then let him say to the family : Let us praise God for all His mercies ; saying,

" Glory be to the Father, and to the Son, and to the Holy Ghost ;

" As it was in the beginning, is now, and ever shall be, world without end." Amen.

Then let him say to the family : Let us pray for God's blessing and protection ; saying,

" Our Father, which art in heaven ;" &c.

And then let him conclude the whole, saying,

" The Grace of our Lord Jesus Christ, and the Love of God, and the Fellowship of the Holy Ghost, be with us all evermore." Amen.

There is not one person but can say these prayers already, and only wants to be put into a method of saying them after this orderly manner ; and I am sure the comfort and blessing of bringing all our people that cannot read to this, would be unspeakably great both to them and to ourselves ; and, for the love of God, let it be attempted in good earnest.

AN

ADMONITION

PROPER FOR

PARENTS.

Most parents are concerned for their children's present welfare, and too often renounce a good conscience rather than not provide for them; while few are careful to give them such instructions and examples, as, by the grace of God, may secure them an eternal inheritance.

They should therefore be often put in mind of their duty in this particular, that they may not have the torment of seeing their children for ever ruined by their negligence.

It is a strange stupidity, and they should be told of it, for parents to be much concerned to have their children dedicated to God in Baptism, and yet utterly unconcerned how they behave themselves afterwards.

The least that parents can do is, To instruct, or get their children instructed, in the principles of the Christian religion;—to pray for them daily, and to see that they pray daily for themselves;—to possess their minds with a love of goodness, and with an abhorrence of every thing that is wicked;—and to take care that their natural corruption be not increased by evil examples.

It is a sad thing to see children, under the very eye of their parents, and too often by their examples, getting habits of vanity, of idleness, of pride, of intemperance, of lying and pilfering, of talebearing, and often of uncleanness, and of many other sins which might be prevented by a Christian education.

Parents, therefore, should be made sensible of their great guilt, in suffering their children to take evil ways. They should be often told, that human nature being extremely corrupt, we need not be taught and be at pains to go to hell; we shall go thither of course, if we do not make resistance, and are not restrained by the grace of God, and our own care and endeavour.

They should know, (however loath they are to hear it,) that they are their children's worst enemies, when they will see no faults in them, —connive at what ought to be corrected,—and are even pleased with what ought to be reproved.

"*He that spareth his rod,*" saith Solomon[p], "*hateth his son;* (that is, acts as if he really did so;) *but he that lovet hhis son, chasteneth him betimes;*" that is, before he grows headstrong, and before he is corrupted by evil habits. For "*a child left to himself bringeth his mother to shame[q].*"

In short, a parent, who has any conscience of his duty, will not suffer the least sin to go unreproved or without due correction; but then he will take the Apostle's advice[r], "*not to provoke their children to wrath,*" by a causeless

p Prov. xiii. 24.   q Prov. xxix. 15.
r Col. iii. 21.

or too great severity; lest they be discouraged, and thereby their children's love, both for religion and for themselves, be lessened.

When children are grown up to years of discretion, parents should be admonished *to fit them for Confirmation;*—a privilege which both parents and children would very highly value, if they were made to understand the worth of it, which of all things a Pastor should take care to explain to them.

In the next place, it would be great charity for a Clergyman to interpose his good offices, (at least to offer his advice,) when parents are about to dispose of their children in marriage, upon mere worldly considerations, and very often for little conveniences of their own, without any regard to their children's future ease and welfare.

It is seldom that either parents or children pray for God's direction and blessing upon an undertaking which is to last as long as life; but run on headlong, as humour, or passion, or worldly interest, lead them, which is the true occasion of so many *indiscreet choices* and *unfortunate marriages*, which a Pastor should prevent as much as may be, by admonishing Christians of their duty in this particular, both publicly and in private conversation.

And when parents are providing for their children, let this consideration be always present with them, both for their own and their children's sake: "*Better is a little with righteousness*, (that is, honestly gotten,) *than great revenues without right*[s]."

When a curse goes along with a portion, it is often the ruin of the whole family. These were the remarkable words of the pious Judge Hales to his children: "*I leave you but little, but it will wear like iron.*"

Lastly; A Pastor's advice would be very seasonable, and should be often repeated, to such parents as are squandering away the inheritance that was left them by their forefathers, and left them in *trust only* for those that should come after them; depriving their children of their right, exposing them to hardships, to temptations, and to curse their memory. Con-

[*] Prov. xvi. 8.

siderations which should make their hearts to ache, and force them to put an end to that idleness and intemperance, which are the occasion of so much sin and mischief.

INSTRUCTIONS

PROPER FOR

YOUNG PEOPLE.

IT is the great misfortune of *youth*, that wanting *experience, judgment,* and very often *friends* capable of giving them good advice, and following the bent of their passions, they love and seek such company and pleasures as serve to strengthen their natural corruption, which, if not prevented by charitable advice, will be their ruin.

And certainly a Pastor has much to answer for, who does not lay hold of every occasion of shewing young people their *danger* and their *duty*.

The first thing a youth should be made sensible of, is this :

That he has in himself the seeds of all manner of sin and wickedness, which will certainly spring up and be his ruin, if he does not watch against it, and pray daily for God's grace to preserve him from it:—That the wickedest man he knows was once as capable of salvation as he thinks himself to be; but by provoking God to leave him to himself, sin and hell have got the dominion over him:— And that therefore it is the greatest judgment that can fall upon any man, *to be left to himself.*

To come to particulars:—

First. Young people are apt to be *head-strong*, and *fond of their own ways*, and should therefore be told what God declares by Solomon[t], "*Poverty and shame shall be to him that refuseth instruction; but he that regardeth reproof shall be honoured.*"—That "*there is a way that seemeth right to a man, but the end thereof are the ways of death*[u]."

Secondly. They love idleness naturally, and therefore should be put in mind,—That "*slothfulness casteth into a deep sleep*[x];" that

[t] Prov. xiii. 18.   [u] Chap. xiv. 12.   [x] Chap. xix. 15.

is, makes men as careless of what will become of them as if they were fast asleep; and that *"drowsiness will cover a man with rags[y]."* Above all, they should be put in mind of our Lord's sentence, *" Cast ye the unprofitable servant into outer darkness."*

Thirdly. This being the age of *sensuality, libertinism,* and *vanity;* it must be a great grace, and very frequent instructions, that must secure young people from ruin.

They should therefore be often told,

That *"fools* (and only fools) *make a mock at sin[z];"* it being too dreadful a thing to be laughed at:

That *"whoredom and wine take away the heart[a];"* that is, make a man a mere brute:

That *" lying lips are an abomination to the Lord[b],"* and that *swearing* and *cursing* are sins easily learned, but hard to be left off, and will be punished most severely:

That *"evil communications will corrupt good manners[c]:"* .

---

y Prov. xxiii. 21.   z Chap. xiv. 9.   a Hosea iv. 11.
b Prov. xii. 22.   c 1 Cor. xv. 33.

That therefore young people should not, at their peril, run into unknown company and temptations, depending upon their own strength and good resolutions.

They should be told,

That nobody is very wicked at once;—that there are few but had some time good notions, good purposes, and good hopes;—and those that are profligately wicked became so after this manner:—they took delight in loose and wicked company;—then they neglected to pray for grace;—then they cast off the fear of God; —then *holiness;*—after that *modesty;*—then care of reputation;—and so, contracting evil habits, they became at last abandoned of God, and left to themselves.

Fourthly. A good Pastor will not forget to exhort young people to "*flee youthful lusts*[d]," and all sins of impurity, filthy songs, and filthy stories, which leave cursed impressions upon the soul, do grieve God's Holy Spirit, which was given them at Baptism and at Confirmation, and provoke Him to forsake them; and

[d] 2 Tim. ii. 22.

then an evil spirit most certainly will take them under his government.

Fifthly. Such as have parents should be exhorted to *love, honour,* and *obey* them. That, as the Apostle saith[x], "*It may be well with them, and that they may live long on the earth.*" That they may escape that curse pronounced[y], "*Cursed is he that setteth light by his father and mother;*"—and that of the Wise Man[z], "*The eye that mocketh at his father, and despiseth to obey his mother, the ravens of the valley shall pick it out;*" that is, such a one shall act in every thing he does as if he were blind.

In short, children, as they hope for God's favour and blessing, should strive to please their parents;—be grieved when they have angered them;—take their advice kindly, and follow it cheerfully; and never marry without their consent, as they hope for happiness in that estate.

Above all things, young people should be obliged to observe the Lord's Day:—They should be taught to reverence God's House,

[x] Eph. vi. 1.　　[y] Deut. xxvii. 16.　　[z] Prov. xxx. 17.

and God's Ministers, who pray for them, and are to give an account for their souls.

They should be exhorted to pray daily for themselves, and against being led away by the violence of evil customs and the ways of the world, which they have renounced at their Baptism.

And when they have run into errors, (which they are but too apt to do,) they should be made sensible of the ruin they are bringing upon themselves, that they may return to a better mind, and, after the example of the prodigal in the Gospel, beg God's pardon, and sin no more; being often forewarned, that God will, one time or other, *"make them to possess the iniquities of their youth*[a]*."*

[a] Job xiii. 26.

OF

WORLDLY-MINDEDNESS.

A PASTOR will find that *worldly-mindedness* is one of the most universal diseases of his flock, and the most difficult to be cured.

People see an absolute necessity of taking care for themselves; and duty obliges them to provide for their families.

But then this care very often increases beyond necessity, and what was at first a duty becomes at last a sin; when Christians begin to set their hearts upon the world, to place their happiness in its favours, to dread its frowns, and to depend upon it as a good security against future evils.

Now, the consequence of such a love for the world will be, that many Christian duties give place to worldly business; the very commands of God shall often be broken to gain worldly ends; men shall make a mere idol of the world; *love*, and *fear*, and *think*, and *depend upon* it, more than upon God, and will at last be so bewitched and blinded with it, that they shall not see the sin and vanity of all this, until the approach of death opens their eyes, and then they see the folly of their choice, but see, too, that it is too late to make a better.

In short, it is hard to live in the world, and not to love it; and nothing in nature can prevent or cure this disorder, but a sincere belief of the Gospel, and a resolute practice of the duties of Christianity.

For the Christian religion lets us know, that while we are in this world, we are in a state of banishment;—that here we have no abiding place;—that God has made our life short, on purpose that we may have no pretence to set our hearts on this world;—that it is a dreadful thing for a man to have his "*portion in this life*[b];"—that a man's true hap-

[b] Psalm xvii.

piness does not consist in the abundance of the things which he possesseth;—and that God hath ordained that all things here shall be uncertain, and full of troubles, that we may be led more easily to *"set our affections on things above, not on things on the earth*[c]*."*

And forasmuch as it is found by sad experience, that the more men have, the more fond they will be of the world, Christians should be often advised to receive its favours with a trembling hand, and to remember, that the more a man has, the more he must account for, the greater danger he is in, and the more pains he must take to preserve himself from ruin;—for it was not for nothing that our Lord said, *"How hardly shall they that have riches enter into the Kingdom of Heaven*[d]*!"*

In short, there is no greater hindrance to piety than the love of the world; God therefore having made that and the care of our souls the great business of our lives, He has bound Himself to take care of us, and that we shall

[c] Col. iii. 2.　　　　[d] Mark x. 24.

want nothing that is necessary for this life.
"*Take no thought*," saith our Lord [e], "*for your
life, what ye shall eat; nor for your body, what
ye shall put on.*"—Does not your heavenly
Father feed the fowls of the air? Does He not
know that "*ye are better than they,*" and "*that
ye have need of these things?*"

Let not, therefore, Christians flatter themselves with the hopes that worldly business
will excuse them from serving God; our Lord
has already told us what sentence such people
must expect [f]: "*not one of those men shall taste
of My Supper.*"—That is, *those* that were so
taken up about their oxen, their fields, and
their worldly business, that they would not
mind their Lord's invitation.

And indeed our Lord tells us, in another
place [g], That the very word of God will be lost
on those whose hearts are full of the cares of
this world, which "*choke the word, and it
becometh unfruitful.*"

But, then, Christians have another way of
deceiving themselves, and that is, with the

e Matt. vi. 25, &c.   f Luke xiv. 24.   g Mark iv. 19.

hopes of reconciling a love for the world with the love of God.

And yet our Lord Christ assures us, that they are as utterly inconsistent as light and darkness; that "*no man can serve two masters*[h];" and that whoever will be "*a friend of the world is the enemy of God*[i]."

To conclude:—All Christians are by their profession obliged *not to love the world.*

They are also obliged to use all proper means to prevent this love, which would otherwise ruin them.

Especially; they are obliged to great watchfulness, and earnest prayers for God's grace to keep them from becoming slaves to the world; —from placing their confidence or happiness in it;—from taking delight in the possession of it; —from distracting cares about it;—from taking unjust ways to better or secure their portion in it;—from being extremely grieved at the loss of it, or unwilling to part with it when God so orders it:—from an hard heart, and a close hand, when the necessities of the poor call for

[h] Matt. vi. 24.　　　[i] James iv. 4.

it. And lastly; from being diverted, by the hurry of this world, from the thoughts of the world to come.

"For what will it profit a man if he should gain the whole world, and lose his own soul [k] *?"* —*" Remember Lot's wife* [l]*."*

k Mark viii. 36.   l Luke xvii. 32.

ADVICE

TO

MEN OF ESTATES.

MEN of estates are but too apt to abuse the advantages they have above others, and they are unwilling to hear of it; they imagine they are above advice, and for that reason they are in most danger.

But whatever they fancy, a good Pastor will shew them their danger and their duty, *" whether they will hear, or whether they will forbear*[m]*."*

Now, such persons being subject to *idleness*, to *intemperance*, and to *bear hard* upon their poor neighbours, they should have prudent hints given them to avoid these sins which do so easily beset them.

[m] Ezek. ii. 5.

That such, for instance, who have plenty without taking pains, may not contract an habit of idleness, which is the parent of infinite evils; (a man that has nothing to do being ready to do any thing that the devil shall tempt him to;)—a dislike to business;—a love of ease;—a dependance upon an estate more than upon God's providence;—running into company to pass away time;—a neglect of family duties;—an evil example to children and servants;—an estate going to ruin for want of God's blessing and an honest care.

And though no man can call such a person to an account for leading an idle and a useless life, yet God often does do it; and hence it is we so often see families of an ancient standing broke, and estates crumbled into pieces, because the owners thereof were above taking pains, and neglected to pray for God's blessing upon their estates and families.

It will be great charity, therefore, however such people will take it, in a Pastor, to put them in mind,

That we are none of us *proprietors*, but only

stewards; for the whole earth is the *Lord's*, and He disposes of it as He pleaseth :

That such as have received more than others, have more to account for:

That if they only seek to please themselves, they may justly fear the sentence of the rich man[n]; "*Remember that thou in thy lifetime receivedst thy good things, for which thou art now tormented.*"

That not only the wicked, but even the *unprofitable* servant, was cast into outer darkness :

That if men have estates, they have greater opportunities of gaining God's favour, by doing good to others :

That if they have more time to spare, they have more time and more reason to serve God :

And if they feel not the afflictions of poverty, they are more obliged to assist and help them that do.

But if, instead of doing so, they consume their estates upon their lusts ; and when,

[n] Luke xvi. 25.

having received more favours from God, they should be examples and encouragers of religion, they become themselves the greatest contemners of religion; if their plenty makes them forget God, and their power more troublesome to their poor neighbours; then an estate is a curse and not a blessing.

In short; those that have estates should be charged, as the Apostle directs[o], "*not to be high-minded; not to trust in uncertain riches, but in the living God; that they do good; that they be rich in good works; ready to distribute, willing to communicate; laying up in store for themselves a good foundation against the time to come, that they may lay hold on eternal life.*"

They should be exhorted to give God thanks for His favours; to lay by a reasonable certain proportion of their incomes, to be bestowed in works of piety and charity; to be examples of industry, sobriety, and godliness, to their children, families, and neighbourhood.

[o] 1 Tim. vi. 17.

CONCERNING THE POOR.

THE poor being God's peculiar care, they ought to have a great share in the concern of His Ministers, to *relieve*, to *instruct*, and to *comfort* them.

For nature being averse to *contempt* and *sufferings*, which are often the lot of poor people, they are therefore too apt to charge God foolishly for the unequal distributions of His providence; so that their minds must be satisfied, and their spirits supported, by such considerations as *these :—*

First;—That Jesus Christ Himself, though Lord of the whole creation, yet made it His choice to be born, and to live in poverty; to convince the poor that their condition is not unhappy, if they do not make it so by their impatience.

Secondly; That there is no state whatever but has its proper difficulties and trials; and the *rich* especially, who are so much envied, are often forced to confess, that, as our Lord has told us, a man's life and happiness "*consisteth not in the abundance of the things which he possesseth*P." And as to the next world, the *poor* have much the advantage of the rich, in wanting so many temptations to the ruin of their souls; and in the less account they have to make for what they have received.

And then the poor (as an excellent poet expresses it)

—— will bless their poverty, who had
No reckonings to make when they are dead.

Thirdly. They should be put in mind, that God has made poverty the lot of many of His dearest servants, fitting them for future and eternal happiness by the short afflictions of this life; weaning their affections from things

P Luke xii. 15.

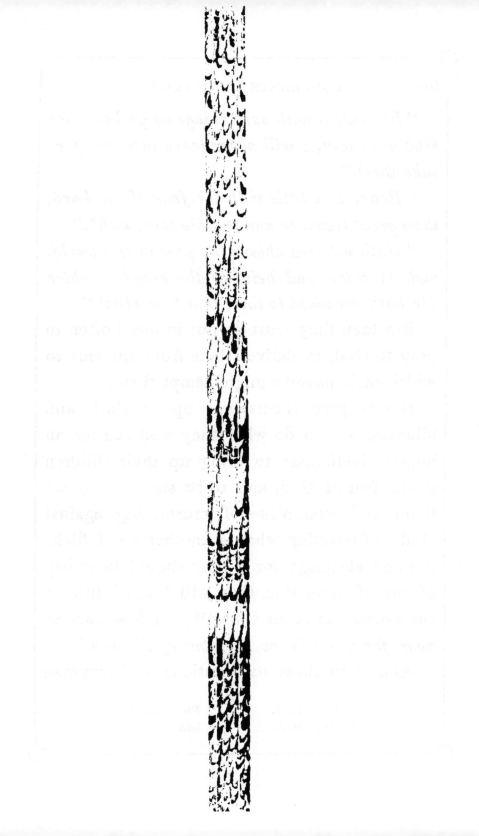

"*Be content with such things as ye have, for God hath said, I will never leave thee, nor forsake thee*[i]."

"*Better is a little with the fear of the Lord, than great treasure and trouble therewith*[k]."

"*Hath not God chosen the poor of this world, rich in faith, and heirs of the kingdom which He hath promised to them that love Him*[l]*?*"

But then they must be put in mind often to pray to God, to deliver them from the sins to which their poverty might tempt them.

Not to give themselves up to sloth and idleness, but to do what they well can for an honest livelihood; to bring up their children in the fear of God, and to be sure not to set them evil examples—of murmuring against God—of coveting what is another's—of filching and stealing: for if they should be guilty of any of these sins, they will lose all title to the promise of Jesus Christ[m]; "*Blessed are ye poor, for yours is the Kingdom of Heaven.*"

And if to these exhortations a Clergyman

* Heb. xiii. 5.   t Prov. xv. 16.
* James ii. 5.   x Luke vi. 20.

PERSONS IN AFFLICTION.

Man (as Job saith[n]) *being born to trouble,* a Pastor can hardly visit his flock, but he will meet with some who will want words of comfort: with which, therefore, he should be always furnished, both to *guide* and to *support* the spirits of the afflicted.

For Christians in affliction are but too apt to distract themselves, and increase their burthen, by considering only what flesh and blood suggest, not what faith and religion propose for their support and comfort.

They are apt to charge God foolishly;—to be angry with those whom He has made or permitted to be the instruments of their af-

[n] Chap. v. 7.

fliction;—to grow dejected and melancholy upon the thoughts of the sins which they suppose have provoked God to visit them;—and lastly, to despair of ever seeing an end to their sorrows.

Here then, the Pastor's help will be seasonable and charitable; for he will teach such as are in trouble to seek comfort in God, and in the aids of religion.

He will convince them, (for instance,)

That events are not left to chance, but that all things come to pass by the appointment or permission of God:

" *That the very hairs of our head are all numbered*[o]:"

That we are under God's care, as well when He suffers us to be troubled, as when He smiles upon us:

That he is a very undutiful child, who will love and obey his father just as long as he pleaseth him, and no longer:

That God has a right to try whether Christians are sincere or not; that is, whether they

[o] Matt. x. 30.

will believe Him to be their God and Father, as well when He corrects, as when He gives them their desires:

That we are in darkness, and do not ourselves know what would be best for us:

That God has made no earthly comforts *full* and *lasting*, on purpose that Christians, seeing the vanity of all worldly enjoyments, may not desire to set up their rest *here*, but be obliged to think of another life, where all tears will be wiped away:

That God often punishes us in this world, that He may not be obliged to punish us hereafter:

That the best of men have need of being awakened into a sense of their duty and danger:

That a disciple of Jesus Christ must take part in the sufferings of his Lord and Master, as he hopes to be a partaker of His glory; *for "if we suffer with Him, we shall also reign with Him*p.*"*

It is thus a Christian may be taught to

p 2 Tim. ii. 12.

submit to God's dispensations, and to make an advantage of what the world calls *misfortunes, afflictions, calamities, judgments.* And that, instead of being *impatient, fretful,* or *dejected,* he should rather rejoice in *tribulation,* in *wrongs,* in *losses,* in *sufferings,* and be glad that he has a proper occasion of offering *his will* a sacrifice to the will of God, which is a most acceptable oblation.

When a Pastor has made his distressed patient sensible of the *reason* and *benefit* of *afflictions,* he will then proceed to shew him how to quiet the disorders of his soul.

He will advise him, (for instance,) not to torment himself about the *cause* of his troubles, or the *instruments* of his afflictions, or be over-anxious concerning the *issue* of them. For this will only create *vexation, fruitless complaints,* and *a sinful distrust,* which are all the effects of *pride* and *self-love,* and serve only to bereave him of that peace of mind, which is necessary to carry him through his trials with the resignation of a Christian.

He will then shew him, that by being

brought into these circumstances, whether his afflictions be for *trial* or *punishment*, he has a special title to the favour of God, and to many great and precious promises, provided he submits to God's order and appointment.   For God has declared Himself to be the Helper of the friendless ; the Comforter of the afflicted ; a *L*ight to them that are in darkness, and know not what way to take.   He has promised to be a Father to the fatherless, and an Husband to the widow ; that He will undertake the cause of the oppressed, and of such as call upon Him in their distress.   So that no man ought to think himself destitute and miserable, who has God to flee to, and God's word for his comfort.

Upon the first *approach* of troubles, therefore, his spiritual guide will direct him to fall down before God,—to humble himself under His afflicting hand,—to acknowledge *that God's judgments are right, and that He of very faithfulness has caused him to be troubled*q; beseeching God that he may make a good use

q Ps. cxix. 75.

of his troubles;—to cast his whole care upon
God, trusting in His wisdom to know, and His
goodness to appoint, what is best for him:
resolving, by the grace of God, to make that
his choice which he has prayed for all his life,
that God's will may be done.

He will also assure him, that, let his mind
be never so much disordered, and his soul
oppressed with sorrow, God can support and
comfort him; that he has a promise of the
same grace which enabled St. Paul to "*take
pleasure in afflictions, in persecutions, in infirmities, in reproaches* [r];" which enabled the first
Christians "*to take joyfully the spoiling of their
goods, knowing that they had in Heaven a better
and an enduring substance* [s];" which enabled
holy Job, under the severest trials, to submit
without repining to God's appointment, saying
only, "*The Lord gave, and the Lord hath taken
away.   Blessed be the Name of the Lord* [t]."

Lastly; his Pastor will tell him, that
St. James is so far from looking upon the case

---

[r] 2 Cor. xii. 10.   [s] Heb. x. 34.
[t] Job i. 21.

of the afflicted as desperate, that he affirmeth, "*Blessed is the man that endureth temptation; for when he is tried*, (that is, *approved*,) *he shall receive a crown of life which fadeth not away* [u]."

And sure no man will think his own case hard, whatever his afflictions may be, when he is put in mind of the sufferings of Christ his Lord and Master, Who had not where to lay His head;—Who was set at nought by those He came to save;—Who was called a dealer with the devil, a glutton, and a wine-bibber;—Who was assaulted by all the powers of hell, so that His soul was sorrowful even to death;—was betrayed by one disciple, and forsaken by all the rest;—was falsely accused by the Jews, set at nought by Herod, unjustly condemned by Pilate, barbarously treated by the soldiers, was led as a sheep to the slaughter, and suffered death, even the death of the Cross.

This was the treatment which the Son of God met with when He was on earth; and this will silence all complaints, or else we are very unreasonable indeed.

[u] James i. 12.

But after all, our greatest comfort is this: That this Jesus, Who Himself was a man of sorrows, and acquainted with grief; Who felt the weakness of human nature, and the troubles to which we are subject: This Jesus is our Advocate with the Father, Who for His sake *"will not suffer us to be tempted above what we are able to bear*[x]*,"* but will enable us, as He did St. Paul, *"in whatever state we are to be therewith content*[y]*."*

"Wherefore, let them that suffer according to the will of God, commit the keeping of their souls unto Him in well-doing, as unto a faithful Creator[z]*."*

[x] 1 Cor. x. 13.   [y] Phil. iv. 11.
[z] 1 Pet. iv. 19.

EXHORTATIONS

PROPER FOR

SERVANTS.

SERVANTS make a considerable part of every Clergyman's charge, and will always stand in need of a particular application. They have as many duties and temptations as other Christians, and have need of as much care—to implant the fear of God in their hearts,—to encourage them to bear with patience the difficulties of their state,—to teach them the duties of their calling,—and to secure them from such sins as they are most subject to.

Servants ought not to imagine, that the meanness of their condition will free them from being accountable to God for their behaviour in that state of life in which His providence has placed them. They are as capable of eternal happiness, and as liable to eternal misery, as the masters they serve; and as strict an account will be required of them. And therefore the Apostles are very particular in setting down the duties of their calling, and the sins they ought to be most careful to avoid.

For example:—That they should be diligent in their business, "*not with eye-service, as men-pleasers, but as the servants of Christ*[a]," "*in singleness of heart, fearing God;—knowing that of the Lord they shall receive a reward*[b]."

They should be often put in mind to make a conscience of their master's interest, that nothing under their care be lost or wasted by *their* negligence. *This is to shew all good fidelity* c.

To be exactly just and honest; not *purloining*, as the Apostle speaks, but remembering, that he was an *unjust steward*, and not to

[a] Eph. vi. 6.   [b] Col. iii. 22. 24.
[c] Titus ii. 10.

be imitated by any honest servant, who made himself friends at his master's cost[e].

To bear with patience the orders and the reproofs of those to whom they are subject, "*not only to the good and gentle, but also to the froward.*" St. Peter saith expressly, that such submission is not only a duty, but a duty *acceptable to God*[f].

They should have a strict charge given them to avoid *lying*, which is hateful to God[g], and *tale-bearing*, which is the occasion of much sin and mischief. Not to corrupt their own or others' hearts and memories with filthy *stories*, wicked *songs*, or profane *expressions*. Never to be tempted by the authority of a wicked master, or by the example of a wicked fellow-servant, to do any thing that is *unjust*, *extravagant*, or any way *unlawful*. To avoid *sloth* and *idleness*, which are very bad characters of a servant.

They should be often called upon to be careful to keep the Lord's Day holy.

Servants have a special right and interest in

Luke xvi. 1, &c. • 1 Pet. ii. 20. [f] Prov. vi. 16.

that day, given them by God Himself,—not to spend it in idleness and vanity, but in going to Church and hearing God's word, and begging His grace, comfort, and blessing, that whatsoever their lot is in this life, they may not fail to be happy in the next.

For this reason, they should be put in mind, that their state of life does not excuse them from praying to God daily as well as they can, that they may faithfully discharge their duty, and patiently bear the burthen laid upon them; which the meanest servant will be better content with, if he is put in mind of our blessed Lord, Who, though He was the Son of the Most High, yet He took upon Him the condition of a servant, to teach us humility, and that the lowest condition is acceptable to God, where people are careful to do the duties of such a state.

Lastly;—Servants should know, that labour is the punishment of sin appointed by God Himself, Who passed this sentence upon Adam[g], "*In the sweat of thy face shalt thou eat*

g Gen. iii. 19.

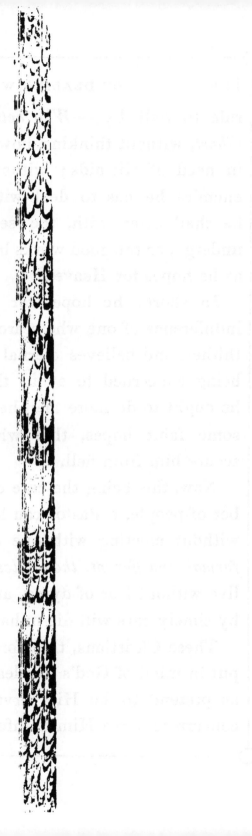

rule to walk by;—*Who believes in the Holy Ghost*, without thinking how much he stands in need of His aids; without considering the enemies he has to deal with, the difficulties he shall meet with, the self-denial he is to undergo, or the good works he must abound in, as he hopes for Heaven.

In short; he hopes for Heaven with the indifference of one who scarce thinks of going thither, and believes eternal torments without being concerned to avoid them. He knows he ought to do more than he does, but he has some faint hopes, that what he does may secure him from hell.

Now, this being the case of an infinite number of people, a Pastor can hardly look abroad without meeting with one or other of these *formal, indifferent, thoughtless* Christians, who live without fear of dying, and if not hindered by timely care will die unhappily.

These Christians, therefore, should be often put in mind of God's displeasure against such as pretend to be His servants, without any concern to serve Him faithfully;—of the folly of being indifferent when a man's soul lies at stake;—of the absolute necessity of an inward conversion, as well as of an outward religion;—of the very great sin of neglecting or abusing the means of grace which God vouchsafes unto us.

He will shew him, moreover, that without a lively faith it will be impossible to please God; —that without a serious repentance there is no forgiveness;—and that *without holiness no man shall see the Lord*[i].

In short; such Christians should have no rest until they shall be forced, out of a sense of their danger, to ask in good earnest, *"What shall I do to be saved?"* until they be prevailed on to consider these words of Christ, *"What shall it profit a man, if he shall gain the whole world and lose his own soul?"* And that it was not for nothing that He commanded His followers—to seek the kingdom of God in the *first* place, and before all other things.

He will then shew him, that all outward Ordinances from the beginning were appointed

i Heb. xii. 14.

either to *create,* or to *promote,* or to *secure,* a lively sense of God, and of the duties we owe Him amongst men.

And as these Ordinances are not at our peril to be neglected, so neither are they to be depended upon, unless they lead us to the love of God, and of our neighbour, and become a means of recovering in us the image of God, in which we were created, which *consists "in righteousness and true holiness* k*."*

When he has convinced them of this, he will exhort them to lose no time, but to beg of God, to increase their *faith,*—to plant His *fear* in their hearts,—to awaken in them an hearty concern for their souls, and to give them such a measure of hope and love of God, as may enable them to overcome the difficulties, the temptations, and the dangers of a Christian life.

And the good Pastor will not fail to add to these endeavours, his own earnest prayers that God of His great mercy would awaken the careless world into a better sense of religion

k Eph. iv. 24.

are for their souls; that men may desire
d earnest to serve God, and be solicitous
o do it most acceptably, without abusing
eans of grace, or deluding themselves
the foolish hopes of serving God and
, of being indifferent here, and happy
ter.

OF

DEALING WITH

HABITUAL EVIL LIVERS.

———

To visit people of this character, when they come to die, is so frightful and so difficult a part of a Clergyman's duty, that one would be at any pains to prevent so afflicting and so uneasy a task; and which can only be prevented by dealing with such people very often and plainly, while they are in health.

By representing to them the danger they are in, while they live in open rebellion against

God : that as sure as God is just, He will call them to a severe account for the abuse of His good creatures,—for defiling their own bodies,—for tempting others to sin,—for mis- spending that very time which God has given them to work out their salvation,—for the evil example they give,—for leading an idle and unprofitable life,—and for dishonouring *God*, His *Laws*, His *Name*, His *Word*, and His *Day*. Upon all which accounts, they are under the displeasure of Almighty God ; His judgments are hanging over their heads continually ; nor have they any hopes of mercy but by a speedy repentance.

For (as it is plain from God's word[l],) the sentence of eternal death is already pronounced against them, and God only knows how soon it may be executed. *Whoremongers, drunkards, unjust, profane*, and even the *unprofitable*, shall not inherit the Kingdom of Heaven, but shall be cast into outer darkness,—"*where the worm dieth not, and where the fire is not quenched*[m]."

[l] Gal. v. 19.   [m] Mark ix. 44.

By doing this faithfully, a Pastor will keep the conscience and the fears of a sinner awake; he will sin at least with uneasiness; and finding that sin is a *real slavery*, he may perhaps at last resolve to seek for ease in the ways of God's commandments.

That he may do so, we ought to set before him the happiness which he is yet capable, by God's grace, of obtaining; for the very design of the Gospel (as Jesus Christ Himself tells St. Paul[n]) is, "*to turn men from darkness to light, and from the power of Satan unto God, that they may receive forgiveness of sins, and an inheritance amongst them that are sanctified by faith in*" Christ Jesus.

After this a Pastor must endeavour to drive him from all his holds of false hopes and vain purposes. For instance,—of repenting time enough hereafter; as if sinners could repent when they please, or as if it were enough to be sorry for one's sins, which a man may be, when it is too late to amend and to "*bring forth fruits meet for repentance*[o]."

[n] Acts xxvi. 18.   [o] Matt. iii. 8.

Let him therefore see that, by deferring his repentance, he makes it still more difficult to repent, and that, when once he has filled up the measure of his sins, he must after *that* expect neither grace nor pardon.

Lest he should depend upon the "*goodness and long-suffering of God*p," let him know that *this* ought to lead him to repentance.

That it is a great mercy that God, notwithstanding all a sinner has done to provoke Him, will yet restore him to favour, and be a Father to him.

Let him know, that there is certainly evil towards that man, who sins and prospers in his sin, it being a sign of God's greatest displeasure, and that He leaves such a man to himself:—a condition the most to be dreaded.

Let him be assured, that if once the sentence of the unfruitful tree be passed, "*Cut it down, why cumbereth it the ground*q?" the prayers and tears of the whole world cannot save it.

And lastly; endeavour to convince him, that God is *just*, as well as *good*, and that He

p Rom. ii. 4.　　　　　q Luke xiii. 7.

has already shewn, that His mercy and goodness can be provoked, since He has condemned
creatures of a much higher and better order
than we are, even the very Angels themselves
when they rebelled, whom *"He hath reserved
in everlasting chains unto the judgment of the
great day*[r]*."*

After this, represent to him the mercy of
God, in sparing him so long, and in not cut-
ting him off in the midst of his sins; His
readiness to forgive such as truly turn unto
Him; and that there is joy in Heaven over a
sinner that repenteth.

And that he may not think his case desperate, (as great sinners are apt to do when
their consciences are awake,) or that it is a
thing impossible to overcome the evil habits
he has contracted; let him understand, that
as the *goodness*, so the *power* of God, is infinite; that the same Spirit which raised up our
Lord Jesus Christ from the dead, can raise a
sinner *"from the death of sin unto a life of
righteousness."*

[r] Jude 6.

This let him stedfastly believe, and use his endeavours, and such a faith will work wonders.

Now, if a sinner is once brought to a sense of his evil condition, and has thoughts of becoming a new man, he will still want his Pastor's assistance and advice, what methods to take in order to his sincere conversion.

And first, he must be told plainly, that he has a work of labour and difficulty to go through; such as will require thoughts of heart, great patience, earnest prayers, and earnest endeavours, self-denial, and perseverance: but then he must consider, *that it is for his life,* and that Jesus Christ has told us, *That "strait is the gate, and narrow is the way, that leadeth unto life*[s].*"

He must then be made sensible, that as of himself he can do nothing, so by the grace of God he can do every thing that God requires of him, which he must pray for with the concern of one that is in earnest.

To his prayers, he must add his best endeavours; that is, he must avoid the occasions

[s] Matt. vii. 14.

of sin;—keep out of the way of temptations; —avoid all company that may any way divert his thoughts from his holy purposes;—he must fast, and deny himself a great many things which his corrupt heart hankers after.

And if these things appear difficult unto him, let him ask himself, whether it is better to do so now, than to "*dwell with everlasting burnings*" hereafter[t]?

A sick man, for his *health*, will do all this: —he will avoid company; he will observe rules; he will take very bitter potions; he will endure very many things to make the remainder of a short life comfortable. A sinner, who considers that his *soul* lies at stake, and that eternal happiness or misery will be the event, will not think any thing too much which God prescribes.

Lastly. If to these pious endeavours a Pastor adds his own prayers for the sinner, that God would touch his heart, take from him all obstinacy and blindness;—that he would awaken him, give him a lively sense of his sad

[t] Isaiah xxxiii. 14.

condition:—call him to repentance, enable him to break all his bonds, graciously forgive him, and give him all those helps that are necessary to become a new creature: a Pastor (whatever is the consequence) will have the comfort of having done a good work, and his duty.

NECESSARY INSTRUCTIONS

FOR SUCH AS ARE UNDER THE

CENSURES OF THE CHURCH.

WHAT the Church of England so passionately wishes for, (namely, that godly discipline may be restored,) this Church, by God's favour, does actually enjoy[u]. "*Notorious sinners are put to open penance, and punished in this world, that their souls may be saved in the Day of the* LORD, *and that others, admonished by their example, may be more afraid to offend.*"

Now to make this a real blessing to our Church and people, it is necessary that they

[u] Commination.

should be often and plainly told the meaning and reason of Church discipline.

They should be told, for instance, that the Church is Christ's family;—that all the members of Christ's family ought to be blameless and holy, as they hope for any reward from Him;—that none are admitted into His household, but such as do solemnly promise to live as becomes His servants;—that therefore such as after this turn disorderly livers, are first to be rebuked, and by fair means if possible brought to reason; if not, to be turned out of His House, till they become sensible of their error; which if they do, and give sincere marks of their repentance, they will be readmitted into the Church, and partake of its privileges as formerly.

Now that all this may be orderly performed, Jesus Christ Himself ordained His Apostles, and gave them power to ordain others, to be the stewards of this His family. To them He gave the keys of His House, with full power to *receive* such as they should find worthy, and to *shut out* the unworthy.

(1) Ministers: that should be made sensible that, as by this, an distance made sensible of Christ's Death and holy, children of God, that to have a right to apply it... deal with the freedom of children, and desire in this Kingdom of Heaven so, by God's promise, they are verily cut off from... privileges, until they...

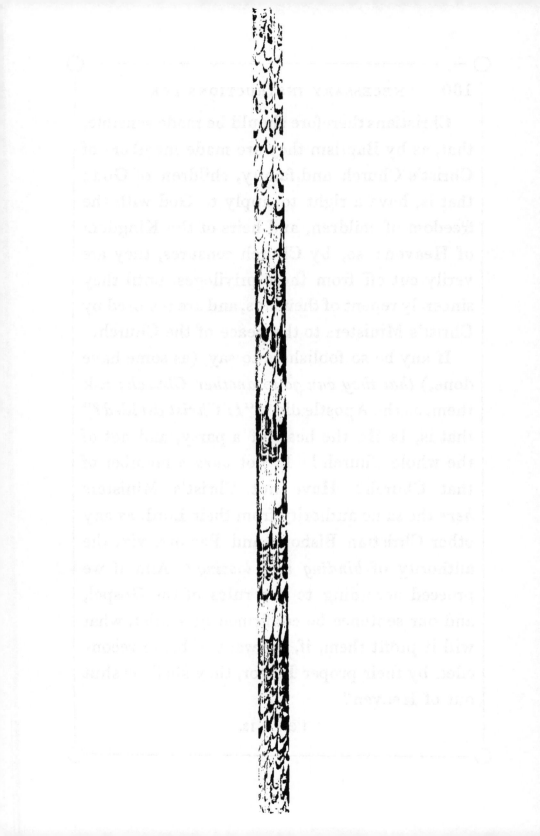

Christians therefore should be made sensible, that, as by Baptism they are made members of Christ's Church and family, children of God; that is, have a right to apply to God with the freedom of children, and heirs of the Kingdom of Heaven; so, by Church censures, they are verily cut off from these privileges, until they sincerely repent of their sins, and are restored by Christ's Ministers to the peace of the Church.

If any be so foolish as to say, (as some have done,) *that they can go to another Church;* ask them, as the Apostle did[z], *"Is Christ divided?"* that is, Is He the head of a party, and not of the whole Church? Is not *ours* a member of that Church? Have not Christ's Ministers *here* the same authority from their Lord, as any other Christian Bishops and Pastors, viz. the authority of *binding* and *loosing?* And if we proceed according to the rules of the Gospel, and our sentence be confirmed by Christ, what will it profit them, if, for want of being reconciled by their proper Pastor, they shall be shut out of Heaven?

1 Cor. i. 13.

Read therefore the commission which Jesus Christ has given us; read it to them out of His word[a]: "*Verily I say unto you, whatsoever ye shall bind on earth,* (proceeding according to the rules of the Gospel,) *shall be bound in Heaven,*" &c. and "*He that receiveth whomsoever I send, receiveth Me*[b]."—"*And whoso despiseth Me, or whomsoever I send, despiseth God that sent Me*[c]."

Let people know, that we take no pleasure in using our authority; that we do not desire to lord it over God's heritage.   Our aim and endeavour is, to oblige sinners to change their course of life, and be converted, that their souls may be saved; and that whenever they give us hopes of a sincere repentance, we receive them with open arms and joyful hearts.

Convince them, that it is not to expose offenders that we oblige them to do public penance, but that they may give glory to God, and declare to all the world, that, since they

---

[a] Matt. xviii. 18.   [b] John xiii. 20.

[c] Luke x. 16.

have been so unhappy as to dishonour God by breaking His laws, and despising His authority, they are heartily sorry for it, and think it no shame to own it after any manner the Church shall order; believing that such a submission to God's Ministers will be acceptable to God Himself, and a means of obtaining His pardon through their intercession.

Assure them that, in the primitive times, Christians begged with prayers and tears to be admitted to public penance, as the only way to obtain the pardon of their sins; they looked upon it as much a favour, as if a man, who had forfeited his life or estate, could have them restored upon acknowledging his crimes and promising amendment.

Lastly; Let them know for certain, that if the Church should not take notice of them, but admit them to her holy Offices and Sacraments, while they continue impenitent, this would be no more a blessing to them than it was to Judas, of whom the devil took more sure possession, after he had received the Sacrament from our Lord's own hands.

By taking pains to instruct penitents (and your people too out of the pulpit) in these particulars,

Offenders will be brought to a sense of their evil condition;—They will perform penance after an edifying manner:

You will promote the honour of God, the good of sinners, the truth of religion, and the public weal, and secure the authority of the Church.

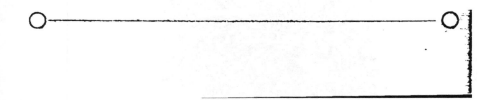

CHARITAS OMNIA SUSTINET

OF

VISITING THE SICK.

IF one seriously considers how the generality of Christians go out of the world; how ill prepared for eternity; and how seldom such as recover make that good use of sickness, which God designs by such visitations; one cannot but wish, that such as have the care of souls would think in good earnest, how to improve such momentous occasions to the best advantage.

And surely a good Pastor must have a great concern upon his spirits, when any of his flock are visited with sickness.

For if the sickness shall be unto death,
here is a soul, in a few days, to enter upon a
state of endless happiness or endless misery:
—A thought which should make one's heart
to tremble.

But if the sick person shall recover, and is
not bettered by his sickness, here is, perhaps,
the *last* opportunity, which God may afford
that man of seeing the error of his ways, for
ever lost; and where the blame will lie, God
Himself has told us[d]: "*He is taken away in his
iniquity, but his blood will I require at the
watchman's hand.*"

Why; what could the watchman do? He
could at least deliver his own soul. But
he must do a great deal more: so saith the
Spirit of God by Elihu[e]: *When a man "is
chastened with pain upon his bed," and "his soul
draweth near unto the grave:" "If there be with
him an interpreter,"* that is, one able to explain
the meaning and use of such visitations; "*If
he say, I have sinned, and it profited me not,*"
that is, if he be brought to true repentance;

d **Ezek. xxxiii. 6.**   e **Job xxxiii. 19—30.**

"*then will God be gracious unto him,*" "*and his soul shall see the light. Lo, all these things worketh God oftentimes with man, to bring back his soul from the pit, to be enlightened with the light of the living.*"

In short; sickness, whether mortal or not, cometh not by chance, but is a warning for men to prepare for eternity. And it mightily concerns such as have the care of souls, not to lose such occasions of doing the greatest good to the souls of men, always remembering, that "*I was sick and ye visited me not*[f]," is one of those reasons for which men will be shut out of Heaven.

Now, the design of this paper is,—To propose a method of answering the ends of the Church in her excellent Office for *Visiting the Sick*. That such as are put into our hands, by the providence of God, may be dealt with as their needs require: whether it be to examine the sincerity of their faith and repentance; or to receive their confession, and administer absolution to such as earnestly desire

f Matt. xxv. 43.

it; or to awaken the consciences of the careless; to comfort dejected spirits; or lastly,
to exhort such as recover, to consider the
mercy they have received, and to dedicate
the remainder of their lives to the service of
God.

And, in the first place, a good Pastor will
not always stay till he is sent for. He knows
that the repentance of the dead comes too late,
and that the fear of death, which is to determine a man's state to all eternity, will make
men willing to hear reproof, and to take advice: such an opportunity, therefore, he will
not lose if he can possibly help it.

They that omit the salutation—P*eace be to
this house and to all that dwell in it*, or pronounce it so low as not to be heard, have not
well considered the authority they have, as
Ministers of Christ, to offer peace and salvation to all that are disposed to receive it[g].

If the *short Litany* and *Prayers following*
be said with deliberation and devotion, there
cannot better be made use of: besides, they are

g Matt. x. 13.

the voice of the Church, which will be sure to be heard at the Throne of Grace.

After these follow *two Exhortations*, which should never be omitted: but then they should be read with very great deliberation, that the sick person may weigh what is said, and receive *instruction* and *comfort* from it.

And now, forasmuch as a well-grounded faith in God will be the sick person's best defence against the assaults of the devil[h], who will be sure to tempt him, either to despair of God's mercy, or to presume upon his own righteousness, or to be impatient, and to charge God foolishly; the Church, therefore, in the next place directs us—*to examine the sick person's faith*, that is, whether he believes as a Christian man ought to do, or no: and in order to that, to ask him,—*Dost thou believe in God the Father Almighty, &c.?*

But lest sick people, and such as are of slow understanding, should profess with their lips, what they are not able to apply to their soul's comfort; it will be highly charitable

h Eph. vi. 16.

and useful, after repeating the Creed, to propose the use that ought to be made of it, *in
short questions*, after some such way as this
following:—

Do you believe that it is God Who ordereth
all things both in Heaven and on earth?

Then you must believe that nothing can
come by chance ; and that, as our Lord saith,
*even a sparrow does not die without God's
knowledge and His leave.*

Do you believe that this present visitation
of yours is from God?

If God is our Father, His correction must
be for our good.

Do you firmly believe this;—and that this
sickness is ordered by Him for some special
end?

Then consider for what ends a loving
father corrects his child; either he is careless, or
disobedient, or forgets his duty ; or takes such
ways as would ruin himself, if he were let alone.

Is not this your case?

To be sure, if it were left to your own
ordering, you would never choose afflictions ;

You must therefore consider wherein you have broke His laws, and you must repent of it, ask God's pardon, and resolve to do so no more, as you hope that He will be a *Saviour to you.*

You believe *that He was conceived of the Holy Ghost, and born of the Virgin Mary?*

Why then you are sure that He is the Son of God, He is able to save such as come unto God by Him; and as He was born of a woman, and took our nature upon Him, He knows, for He has felt, our weaknesses, and will pity our infirmities.

You believe *that He suffered under Pontius Pilate, was crucified, dead, and buried.*

Are you not then hereby convinced what a sad state man was in, when God could not be reconciled to him, till His own Son had suffered what man had deserved to suffer?

And do not you see, at the same time, that no true penitent need despair, since here is a sufficient price paid for our redemption?

Neither ought you to doubt that God will

deny us any thing, since "*He spared not His own Son, but gave Him up for us all*i."

Do you therefore place all your hopes of mercy in Christ's death, and in the promises of God, for His sake, made to us?

Will you endeavour to follow the example of your Lord and Saviour, Who bore with submission and patience whatever God thought fit to lay upon Him?

And will you remember, that He did so, though His very judge found no fault in Him? *But we suffer "justly, for we receive the due rewards of our deeds*k."

And lastly; you will do well to remember the dying words of our Saviour; and when you come to die, *commend your spirit into the hands of God*l.

———

You believe *that Jesus Christ rose again the third day from the dead.*

Why then you are sure, that His sufferings

i Rom. viii. 32. k Luke xxiii. 41. l Luke xxiii. 46.

and death were well-pleasing to God, Who otherwise would not have raised Him to life again.

And though your soul, when you die, shall go into an unknown world; yet, if you die in the favour of God, you will have the same God to take care of you that Jesus Christ had.

And lastly; you are hereby assured, that God, "*Who raised Christ from the dead, will also quicken our mortal bodies*[m];" for so He hath declared in His word.

Since you believe *that Jesus Christ ascended into Heaven, and sitteth at the right hand of God*, you must conclude, that "*all power in Heaven and in earth*[n]" is committed unto Him.

And can there be greater comfort for a sinner than this: That He Who died for us is ever with God, pleading the cause of His poor creatures that come unto God by Him?

Though therefore, for your own sake, you cannot look for favour, yet for Jesus' sake you may, "*Who ever liveth to make intercession for us*[o]."

---

[m] Rom. viii. 11.   [n] Matt. xxviii. 18.   [o] Heb. vii. 25.

Will you therefore endeavour to set your heart above, where your Saviour is?

And that you may do so more earnestly, remember your Saviour's words when He was leaving the world:—"*I go to prepare a place for you, that where I am, ye may be also.*"

———

You believe *that Jesus Christ shall come to judge both the quick and the dead.*

If you believe this so truly as you ought to do, you will take care to judge yourself beforehand, that you may not be condemned of the Lord, when He cometh to judge the world in righteousness.

Will you therefore examine your life, and see wherein you have offended, that you may repent and make your peace with God, remembering, that as death leaves you, judgment will find you?

However, you have this to comfort your soul, if you are sincerely penitent, that He who knows our infirmities, He who died to redeem us, is to be our Judge.

And God grant that you may find mercy in that great Day.

———

You profess to *believe in the Holy Ghost*, to whom you were dedicated in Baptism, and by whom you were "*sealed to the day of redemption*[1]."

Now, if you have *grieved* this Holy Spirit, and by wicked works have driven Him from you, you must sadly repent of it, and earnestly pray to God to restore Him, without whose aid, you can never be sanctified, never be happy.

And when you call yourself to an account, consider whether you have lived in obedience to those *whom the Holy Ghost hath set over you;* that is, the Ministers of the Gospel.

Do you purpose to live and die *in the communion of this Church* in which you were baptized?

[1] Eph. iv. 30.

Our Lord tells you what a blessing it is to be a member of that Church, of which He is the Head.—"*I am* (saith He) *the Vine, ye are the branches; as the branches cannot bear fruit unless they abide in the vine, no more can ye, unless ye abide in Me*ᵐ."

In short, a member of Christ's Church has a right to the forgiveness of sins,—to the favour of God,—to the merits of Christ,—to the assistance of the Holy Ghost,—and to the ministry of the holy Angels. Blessings which you can never be sufficiently thankful for.

———

Do you firmly believe, that God, in consideration of Christ's sufferings, will forgive all such as with hearty repentance and true faith turn unto Him?

But then you must consider, that *forgiveness of sins* is to be hoped for only in God's own way; that is, by the ministry of those to

ᵐ John xv. 5.

whom God has committed the word of reconciliation.

And that the promise of forgiveness of sins
*should be no pretence for continuing in sin in
hopes of pardon.*

———

Do you believe that we shall all rise again,
some to *everlasting happiness*, and some to
everlasting misery?

If this faith be in you of a truth, it will convince you of the vanity of this world, its pro-
fits, pleasures, honours, fame, and its idols;
so that you will not, as unbelievers do, look
for your portion here.

Do not you see what a mercy it is when
God punisheth sinners in this life, since they,
whose punishment is deferred till the next,
must suffer everlastingly?

And if the difficulties of repentance and an
holy life affright you, consider this one thing,
Who can dwell with everlasting burnings?

Remember the words of Christ to the penitent thief: " *This day shalt thou be with Me in Paradise.*"

Let the expectation of that happy day, and a faith and hope full of immortality, make you diligent to make your calling and election sure, and sweeten all the troubles and difficulties of doing it.

And may Almighty God strengthen and increase your faith, that you may die in this belief, and in the peace and communion of the Church. *Amen.*

———

The sick Christian having thus professed his *faith in God*, the next thing necessary to be inquired into is, *the Truth of his Repentance.* The Church therefore orders, that now the Minister shall *examine* (not *exhort* him to it only) whether he repent him truly of all his sins?

And verily the Church in *this* consulted the necessities of *sick persons*, who are not able to attend to long exhortations, and are too apt

to forget what is said to them after that manner; and may be brought to know the true
state of their souls by *examining* them, that is,
by short, plain, and proper questions; of
which hereafter.

In the mean time, a prudent Pastor will
find himself obliged (here) to consider more
particularly the circumstances of the person
with whom he has to do, that he may examine
his repentance accordingly.

For instance, Christians are not always
sensible of their own ailments.

First. Some are very *ignorant,* and know
not why they live, or what will become of
them when they die.

Secondly. Some are *vainly confident,* and
must be humbled.

Thirdly. Some are *too much dejected,* and
must be comforted.

Fourthly. Some are *hardened,* and must be
awakened.

Fifthly, and lastly. Such as hope to recover
will be apt to *put off their repentance,* and
reject the counsel of God for their good.

Now, something in all these cases should be said, to dispose the sick to a sincere repentance.

1. *To such as are very ignorant.*

Such as are *ignorant* should be made sensible, that this life is a state of trial, and a passage only to another.

That God has given men reason and consciencè, and has also given them laws to walk by.

That after this life we must all appear before the Judgment-seat of Christ, " *Who will render to every man according to his deeds*[n]."— *That such as have done good, shall go into life everlasting; and such as have done evil, into everlasting misery.* And that thus it will be, whether men lay these things to heart or not.

And the only comfort a sinner has is this, that God for Christ's sake will accept his sincere repentance.

[n] Rom. ii. 6.

I require you therefore, as you value your soul, to make your peace with God speedily. And that you may know wherein you have offended, I will set before you the law of God, to the end you may judge yourself, and call on God for mercy, as often as I shall put you in mind of any sin you have been guilty of.

2. *To such as are vainly confident.*

Such as are *confident* of their own righteousness, or depend upon an outward profession of Christianity, should be put in mind of our Lord's words to the Pharisees°: "*Ye are they that justify yourselves before men, but God knoweth your hearts.*"

They should be told, that the Publican who durst not lift up his eyes to Heaven, but smote upon his breast, saying, "*God be merciful unto me a sinner,*" returned justified before him who thought too well of himself.

° Luke xvi. 15.

And that our Lord invited such only as were weary and heavy laden to come to Him, because these only are prepared to become His true disciples.

"*Thou sayest, that thou art rich and hast need of nothing,* (saith our Lord to the Church of Laodicea,) *and knowest not that thou art wretched, and miserable, and poor, and blind, and naked*P."

You see how sad a thing it is to have too good an opinion of one's self.

And it is only because Christians do not consider the many duties that they have omitted, and the many sins they have been guilty of, that makes them speak peace to their souls.

In the laws of God, therefore, which I am going to set before you, you will see, as in a glass, the charge that is against you, and I require you to judge yourself, as you expect favour from God.

p Rev. iii. 17.

3. *To such as want comfort, being dejected.*

And first; If the sick person be under agonies of mind, on account of some great sin or wickedness long lived in, a prudent Pastor will not too hastily speak peace to him; he will rather endeavour that he may continue to sorrow after a godly sort; that is, not so much for having offended against a God who can destroy both body and soul in hell, but as having offended a gracious Father, a merciful Saviour, and an holy Spirit.

Such a sorrow as this will not lessen a Christian's horror for sin, but will make him more humble, more fearful of offending; acknowledging God's justice, and his own unworthiness, but yet resolving to lay hold of the promises of mercy, for Christ's sake to penitent sinners.

But then, there being *a sorrow that worketh death*, making sinners impatient, doubting God's goodness, questioning His promises, neglecting repentance; such a sorrow is to be resisted, and discouraged, as a temptation of the devil, being the effect of pride, and of an unwillingness to submit to God.

But if the sick person's sorrow proceed, as it too often does, from mistakes concerning God; the extent of Christ's sufferings; the unpardonableness of some sins and some states; the sincerity of his own faith and repentance; he is then to be comforted with such truths as these:—

That God "*delighteth in mercy* [q]."

That He is "*gracious and merciful, abundant in goodness and truth, forgiving iniquity, and transgression, and sin* [r]."

That the devil, knowing this, uses all his arts and endeavours to tempt sinners to despair.

That therefore God Himself bids us to "*call upon Him in time of trouble, and He will hear us* [s]."

Nay, He calls Himself *a Father*, on purpose that sinners may consider how a father would deal with his own child, when he saw him truly sensible of his errors.

[q] Mic. vii. 18.   [r] Exod. xxxiv. 6, 7.   [s] Ps. l. 15.

That Jesus Christ came into the world to save sinners[t], even such as were lost[u]: That He ever liveth to make intercession for us[x].

And we have His own promise for it:—"*He that cometh unto Me, I will in no wise cast out[y];*" and "*he that believeth in Him shall receive remission of sins[z].*"

That the Gospel is a most *gracious dispensation,* requiring only such an obedience as a poor frail creature can pay.

That that *faith* is not to be questioned which "*purifieth the heart[a];*" "*which worketh by love[b];*" that is, makes us do what we can to please God; and which resisteth temptations, and enables us to overcome them.

That wherever amendment of life followeth such a faith as this, *there is true repentance:* and that where there is sincerity, there our obedience will be accepted, though it be not perfect as the law requires.

In short; no man will have reason to despair, if he considers, *that God doeth nothing*

[t] 1 Tim. i. 15.   [a] Matt. xviii. 11.   [x] Heb. vii. 25.
[y] John vi. 37.   [z] Acts x. 43.   [a] Acts xv. 9.
[b] Gal. v. 6.

in vain: and that if He visits a sinner; if He exhorts him by His Ministers; if He touches his heart; if He gives him time to consider his ways, when He might have taken him away without warning; why, it is because He designs to be gracious, if the sinner is not wanting to himself.

I will therefore set before you the law of God, not to *affright* you, but that you may *know, and confess, and forsake your sin, and find mercy, as God hath promised* [c].

4. *To such as are hardened in wickedness, and must be awakened.*

This is indeed a melancholy case; but a good Pastor, while God continues life, will continue his endeavours, for he does not know but *this* is God's time.

He will therefore try what the *sword of the Spirit* will do, that *word* which, the same *Spirit* tells us, is *profitable for correction as well as for instruction* [d].

[c] Prov. xxviii. 13. [d] 2 Tim. iii. 16.

He will therefore put him in mind, that if he dies in his sins unrepented of, he will go out of the world a professed enemy to that *God* "*Who can destroy both body and soul in hell;*" Who will, as the Holy Scriptures assure us, take "*vengeance on all them that know not God, and that obey not the Gospel of our Lord Jesus Christ,*" "*who shall be punished with everlasting destruction*[e]."

He will let him know, that this may be his condition in a few days; for our Lord assures us, that as soon as ever the wicked man died, he was carried to hell[f].

That this is the last time, perhaps, that ever God will afford you to beg His pardon; and you will be desperately mad to neglect it.

It is true, God is not willing that any should perish, and He can conquer the stubbornest heart, but He will not do it by force.

He has shewn His mercy in afflicting your body, and in taking from you the power to do evil.

What is this for, but that you may open

[e] 2 Thess. i. 8, 9.   [f] Luke xvi.

your eyes, and see your danger, and ask His pardon, and beg His assistance, and be delivered from the severity of His wrath, which you must certainly feel without a speedy repentance?

It may be, you do not know *the charge that is against you;* I will, therefore, repeat to you the substance of those laws which you have broken, and by which you must be judged.

If you have any concern for your soul, if you have any fear of God in your heart, you will hear, and judge, and condemn yourself, that you may escape in the dreadful judgment of the last Day.

5. *To such as, in hopes of recovery, put off their repentance.*

Such should be made sensible,—That sickness is not only the *punishment*, but the *remedy of sin*[g].

That it is the chiefest of those ways, by which God shews men their sin,—by which He discovers to them the vanity of the world

[g] Micah vi. 9.

which bewitches them,—by which He takes down the pride of the heart, and the stubbornness of the will, which have hindered their conversion.

In short; it is God's time: so that not to repent in sickness is in effect to resolve never to repent.

For what shall incline a man to repent when he recovers, which does not move him now?

His hopes of Heaven, and his fears of hell, will not be greater then than now.

And it would be the highest presumption to expect that God will give that man an extraordinary degree of grace, who despises the most usual means of conversion.

A Pastor, therefore, will set before him the law of God, which he has transgressed, that he may see the need he has of repenting, and that he may not provoke God to cut him off before his time, because there is no hope of amendment.

EXAMINATION

OF THE

SICK PERSON'S REPENTANCE.

DEARLY beloved, you are, it may be, in a very short time, to appear before God.

I must therefore put you in mind, that your salvation depends upon the truth of your repentance.

Now, forasmuch as you became a sinner by breaking the laws of God, you have no way of being restored to God's favour, but by seeing the number and the greatness of your sins, that you may hate them heartily, lament them sorely, and cry mightily to God for *pardon*.

I will therefore set before you the laws of God, by which God will judge you; and I will ask you such questions as may be proper to call your sins to your remembrance; and you will do well, wherever you shall have reason, to say with the Publican,—*God be merciful unto me,* for I have offended in *this* or *this thing.*

And be not too tender of yourself; but remember, that the more severe you are in accusing and condemning yourself, the more favour you may expect from God.

———

Your duty to God, you know, *is, to fear Him, to love Him, to trust in Him, to honour, and to obey Him.*

Consider, therefore, seriously;—Have you not lived as if there were no God to call you to an account?

Has the knowledge of God's almighty power, and severe justice, made you fearful of offending Him?

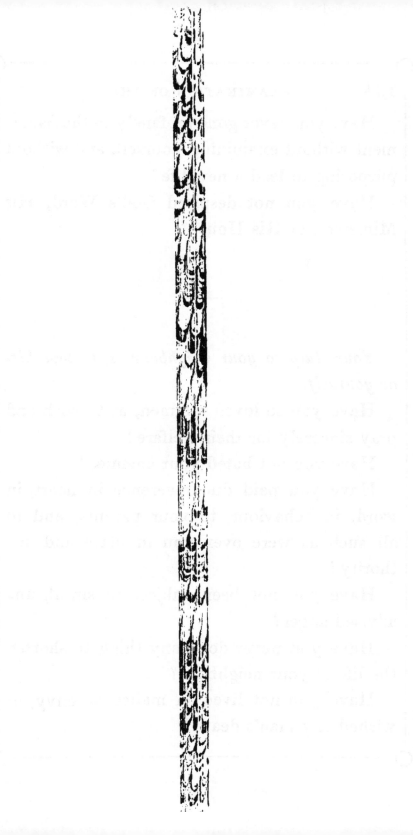

Have you never gone profanely to the Sacrament without examining yourself, and without purposing to lead a new life?

Have you not despised God's Word, His Ministers, or His House?

———

Your duty to your neighbour is, to love him as yourself.

Have you so loved all men, as to wish and pray sincerely for their welfare?

Have you not hated your enemies?

Have you paid due reverence in heart, in word, in behaviour, to your parents, and to all such as were over you in place and authority?

Have you not been subject to sinful, unadvised anger?

Have you never done any thing to shorten the life of your neighbour?

Have you not lived in malice or envy, or wished any man's death?

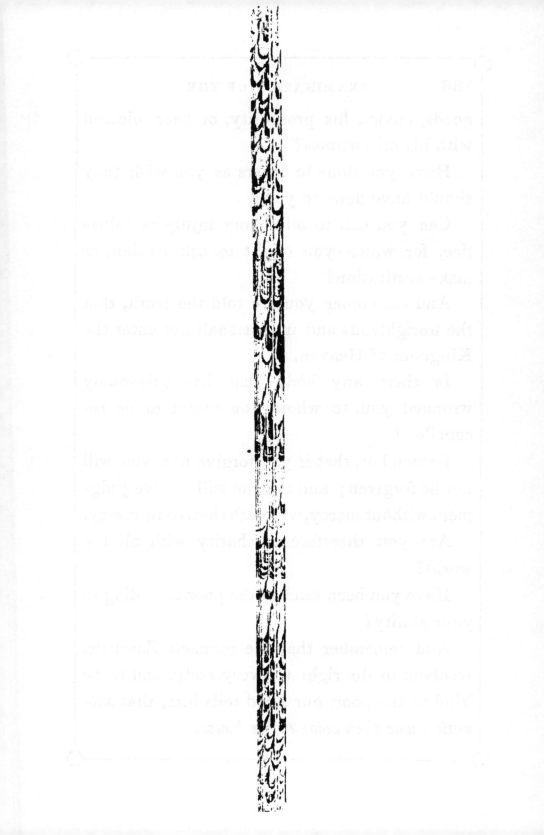

goods, advice, his property, or have played with his ill-humour?

Have you done to others as you with they should have done to you?

Can you call to mind any injury or injustice, for which you ought to ask pardon, or and restitution?

And remember you are told the sixth, that the unrighteous and ... shall not enter the Kingdom of Heaven,

Is there any individual you have grievously wronged, to whom you ought to be more useful?

Remember, that if you ... forgive men, you will not be forgiven; and that the will ... have judgment without mercy, ... shewn no mercy. Are you exercise charity with all the world?

Have you been unkind ... pure and ... to your charity?

and remember that the utmost Zeal in ... conduct in do right and every body, and in find in the poor, our ... it tells him, that such with not one flew away ... home.

goods, envied his prosperity, or been pleased with his misfortunes?

Have you done to others as you wish they should have done to you?

Can you call to mind any injury or injustice, for which you ought to ask pardon, or make restitution?

And remember you are told the truth, that the unrighteous and unjust shall not enter the Kingdom of Heaven.

Is there any body that has grievously wronged you, to whom you ought to be reconciled?

Remember, that if you forgive not, you will not be forgiven; and that he will receive judgment without mercy, who hath shewed no mercy.

Are you therefore in charity with all the world?

Have you been kind to the poor according to your ability?

And remember that the moment Zaccheus resolved to do right to every body, and to be kind to the poor, our Lord tells him, that *salvation was then come to his house.*

You would do well, therefore, as a proof of your thankfulness to God, to be liberal to the poor, according to your ability.

And if you have not already settled your worldly concerns, and declared what you owe, and what is owing to you; it is fit you do so now: for the discharging a good conscience, and for preventing mischief after your death.

And be very careful that in making your will, you do no wrong, discover no resentment, that the last act of your life may be free from sin.

And now I will leave you for a while to God, and to your own conscience; beseeching Him to discover to you the charge that is against you; that you may know, and confess, and bewail, and abhor, the errors of your life past; that your sins may be done away by His mercy, and your pardon sealed in Heaven, before you go hence and be no more seen.

BEATI PAUPERES ANIMO.

CONCERNING

CONFESSION AND ABSOLUTION.

—

CONCERNING Confession, Archbishop Usher has these words:—"No kind of Confession, either public or private, is disallowed by our Church, that is in any way requisite for the due execution of the ancient power of the keys, which Christ bestowed on the Church[d]."

Concerning Absolution, Bishop Andrews hath these words:—"It is not said by Christ, *Whose sins ye wish and pray for, or declare to be remitted;* but *Whose sins ye remit;* to which He addeth a promise, that He will

[d] Answer to the Jesuit, p. 84.

make it good, and that His power shall accompany the power He has given them, and the lawful execution of it in His Church for ever."

And indeed the very same persons Baptize for the remission of sins; and administer the Lord's Supper as a seal of the forgiveness of sins to all worthy Communicants.

It is not water that can wash away sin, nor bread and wine; but these rightly administered, by persons truly authorized, and to persons duly qualified by faith and repentance. And thus Absolution benefiteth, by virtue of the power which Jesus Christ has given His Ministers[e].

In short; our Lord having purchased the forgiveness of sins for all mankind, He hath committed the ministry of reconciliation to us; that having brought men to repentance, we may in Christ's Name, and in the Person of Christ[f], pronounce their pardon.

And this will be the true way to magnify the power of the keys, which is so little understood,

---

[e] John xx. 23.   [f] 2 Cor. ii. 10.

or so much despised; namely, to bring as many as possibly we can to repentance, that we may have more frequent occasions of sealing a penitent's pardon by our ministry.

And now, if the sick person has been so dealt with as to be truly sensible of his condition, he should then be instructed in the nature and benefit of Confession, (at least of such sins as do trouble his conscience,) and of Absolution.

For instance; He should be told that, as under the law of Moses, God made His Priests the judges of leprosy[g], and gave them rules, by which they were to determine who were clean, and fit to enter into the congregation, (which was a type of Heaven,) and who were not clean;—

Even so, under the Gospel, He has given His Priests authority to judge sin, which is the leprosy of the soul. He has given them rules to judge by, with authority to pronounce their pardon, if they find them qualified; for this is their commission from Christ's own mouth,

g Levit. xiii.

"*Whosoever sins ye remit, they are remitted unto them.*"

But then we dare not take upon us to exercise this authority, until sinners give such signs of a sincere faith and true repentance, as may persuade one charitably to believe, that amendment of life will follow, if God shall think fit to grant them longer time.

At the same time, therefore, that we are bound to encourage penitents earnestly to desire Absolution, and to exhort them to receive the Lord's Supper, as a pledge to assure them of pardon; we must sincerely admonish them not to hope for any benefit either from the one or the other, but upon condition of their sincere repentance.

It will be proper, therefore, before Absolution, and for more satisfaction, to ask the sick person some such *questions as these:*

Have you considered the sins which you have been most subject to?

Are you convinced that it is an evil thing and bitter to forsake the Lord?

Are you resolved to avoid all temptations,

and occasions of the sins you have now repented of?

Do you verily believe that you shall not
fall into any of these sins again?

If you should do so, will you immediately
beg God's pardon, and be more watchful over
yourself?

Will you strive with all your might to
overcome the corruptions of your nature, by
prayers, by fasting, and by self-denial?

Do you purpose, if God shall prolong your
days, to bring forth fruits meet for repentance?

Are you in perfect charity with all the
world?

Every Christian, whose life has been, in
the main, unblameable, and whose repentance
has thus been particularly examined, and who
has given a satisfactory answer to these questions, ought not to leave the world without
the benefit of Absolution, which he should be
earnestly pressed to desire, and exhorted to
dispose himself to receive, as the Church has
appointed.

CONCERNING

HABITUAL SINNERS.

IF a person of this character be visited with sickness, a prudent Pastor will not presently apply comfort, or give him assurances of pardon; he will rather strive to increase his sorrow to such a height, as, if God should spare him, might produce a repentance not to be repented of.

It was thus (as Dr. Hammond observes) that God Himself dealt with such kind of sinners [h].

The children of Israel did evil again, that is, they went on in their wickedness, upon

[h] Judges x. 6.

which God sorely distresses them. They cried unto God, but He answers them, *"I will deliver you no more."* However, this did not make them utterly to despair; for they knew that His mercy had no bounds; they therefore still went on to apply to Him for pardon and help, and resolved to do what was *at present* in their power toward a reformation; at last God was prevailed on to accept and deliver them.

And thus should we deal with habitual sinners:—we should not break the bruised reed;—we should indeed give them assurances of pardon, upon their sincere repentance: but forasmuch as it is very hard, even for themselves to know, whether their sorrow and resolutions are such as would bring forth fruit answerable to amendment of life: all that a confessor can do is, To exhort such persons to do all that is in their present power;—to take shame to themselves;—to give glory to God in free confession of their crimes, (which St. James saith is of great use towards obtaining their pardon;)—to pray without ceasing;

—to warn others to beware of falling into the same sad condition;—and to consider that a wicked life, to which God has threatened eternal fire, cannot be supposed to be forgiven by an easy repentance.

And though the Church has no rules in this case to go by, but such as are very afflicting, yet God is not tied to rules; He sees what is in man, and may finally absolve one whom His Ministers dare not, until after a long probation they have reason, in the judgment of charity, to believe that his repentance is sincere.

And this a prudent Pastor will be careful to observe, both to prevent the scandal of an hasty Absolution, and because he knows such ministrations do no good to those that receive them.

TO SUCH AS HAVE

RECOVERED *F*ROM SICKNESS.

———

AND, in the first place, a Pastor should be very careful to put his people in mind, that the first-fruits of health should always be offered to God.

And forasmuch as there is nothing more common, nor more to be lamented, than for people in sickness to make very solemn promises of better obedience, and upon their recovery to forget all, and to return to their former careless life;—a Pastor will warn them betimes, how God hates such backslidings, how unthankful, how provoking it is, and the very readiest way to draw down a worse evil, or to be given over to a reprobate mind.

And, indeed, a man that has received the sentence of death in himself,—that has seen the hazard of a death-bed repentance,—that has felt the horror of sin, when it is most frightful:—for such a person to grow secure, is an amazing instance of the corruption of our nature; and therefore it will require a Pastor's greatest care to prevent a relapse. Especially to guard his people against general purposes of amendment, which lull the mind asleep; and before people are aware, they are just where they were before sickness seized them.

A love for sin returns; God is provoked, and grace withdrawn; and every relapse makes a Christian's case more desperate.

A Christian, therefore, who is in good earnest, must be put upon rectifying the errors of his life, immediately, as he hopes for mercy, whenever God visits him again.

If an idle life has been his fault, he must take to business;—if intemperance, he must at his peril be sober;—if he has been given to appetite, to ease, and to luxury, he must deny himself, and labour to mortify these corrupt affections;—if he has observed no method of living, he must for the future fix proper times for prayer, for fasting, for retirement, and for calling himself to an account.

In short; he must avoid, as much as possible, all occasions and temptations to sin;—if he is overtaken in a fault, he must immediately repent of it, and be more careful; he must *not* be discouraged with the difficulties he will meet with, for the power of God is sufficient to make a virtuous life *possible*, *easy*, and *pleasant*, to the weakest Christian that depends upon His grace.

Let him therefore be exhorted to persevere in his good resolutions;—to depend upon God's power and promises, to assist him to pray dàily for light to discover, and for strength to overcome the corruptions of his nature;—and lastly, to be always afraid of backsliding :—and then sickness and death, whenever they come, will be a blessing.

And as a faithful discharge of this duty will give a Curate of souls the greatest comfort at the hour of death, so there is nothing doth more preserve the authority which a faithful Pastor ought to have over his flock.

INSTRUCTIONS

FOR AN

ACADEMIC YOUTH.

INSTRUCTIONS

FOR AN

ACADEMIC YOUTH.

———

I DO not design, that the following directions should interfere with the Academic Master's business or instructions; I would only give you some few hints, how to fill up, most usefully, the spare hours you may have from the useful studies which he will put you upon.

For though the circumstances of this place do not necessarily require so large a compass of knowledge in Philosophy, as do those of other nations; yet Logic, Metaphysics, and Ethics, and an insight at least into Mathematics, Geography, Astronomy, and Natural Philosophy, will be necessary; not only as they are great helps to the study of Divinity, but as they will set you above the level of the common people; not to elate you with pride, but to make you justly esteemed. The Academic Master will give you the best directions what books to read, and what time to spend on these studies.

But forasmuch as you purpose to dedicate your life and labours to the more immediate service of God, it is fit you should have an eye to that in all your other studies; and it is for this reason I put these short directions into your hands.

And in the first place lay this down for a certain truth, that without God's especial blessing, your best purposes, and all your endeavours, will come to nothing. *"We have toiled all the night, and have taken nothing,"* will be found true by every body who will be making experiments, how far their own natural parts will carry them without the aid of God's good Spirit.

The Divine Grace is necessary for every man, but much more for one who hopes to be instrumental in saving others as well as himself. Let me therefore advise and conjure you, as you hope for success in your studies, to beg of God a blessing upon yourself and labours, every day of your life.

And because there never was, nor ever can be, a good Divine without a good acquaintance with the Holy Scriptures; be persuaded to lay yourself under an obligation of reading every day one chapter at least in the New Testament, with such parts of the Old as the New refers to.

If you are master of the small *Folio* Bible, printed within these few years at Dublin, (which, if well chosen and well bound, will last your whole life,) you have in the margin Dr. Scattergood's and the late Bishop of Worcester's references; which, if you carefully consult and compare, you will come to a competent understanding of the Scriptures, and gain such a knowledge as will stick by you; because gained by your own industry, and God's blessing upon your pains.

At the end of that Bible, you will find a Chronological Table of the Bishop of Worcester's, which you should read over, at spare times, so often, till you are master of it; by which you will have a distinct knowledge of all that passed in the world from the creation till the close of the New Testament, and the order of the several great events in point of time; which will be of greater use to you than at present you can imagine.

There are two things which I do most earnestly recommend to you, as you hope to benefit yourself, or others, by reading the Holy Scriptures. The *first*, that you always implore the assistance of that Spirit by which they were written, for the true understanding of them; and the *second*, that you apply every Scripture as spoken to yourself. For instance, say to yourself; This is the very word of God;—this is *His* command to *me*; it is what He requires of me ;—this, by the grace of God, I will observe. Do I live like one who believes this truth ? Do I act according to this rule ? &c.

Give me credit :—By this plain and easy method, of considering every truth as concerning yourself, your graces will increase with your knowledge :—You will become every day more humble, more devout, more patient, &c. You will avoid the vices, and the snares, there set down, and dread the consequence of falling into them. In one word ; you will come to such a knowledge of divine truths, as that you will know your own duty perfectly ; and in God's good time, be able to teach others.

And indeed this is the very way prescribed by our *Lord* Himself, for arriving at divine knowledge [o] : Εἀν τις θέλη τὸ θέλημα αὐτοῦ ποιεῖν : *If any man will do* (that is, wills, desires to do) *the will of God, he shall know of the doctrine whether it be of God.*

Some books of *piety* and *devotion* you cannot

[o] John vii. 17.

be without. I consider your circumstances; and for the present, I recommend three only of the first kind; namely, *The Whole Duty of Man*, which I take for granted you have already;—*Mr. Law of Christian Perfection*, one of the best books that has appeared in this age;—and a little book entitled *The Life of God in the Soul of Man.*

But then I would have you read these so often, and with care, till your heart be possessed with that spirit by which they were composed. For be assured of it, that two or three books read with care, and often, well understood, and thoroughly digested, will improve you more than two or three hundred read carelessly, and only to gratify your curiosity.

For your private prayers, the *Enchiridion Precum,*—which I have always recommended to scholars that are able and willing to make use of them,—will answer all the ends of devotion, being written in a fine Latin style, and full of quotations out of Holy Scripture; and will at once improve your learning and devotion.

The Greek Testament should be read daily; a chapter every afternoon. This is necessary both to preserve and increase your knowledge in that language in which that book was originally written; and will give you a better understanding in that part of Scripture.

There is another exercise which I would put you upon; and to recommend it more effectually, and that it may not be too rashly censured, I do tell you, it is the advice of one of the greatest men of this age, to the youths in the University; especially to such as are designed for the Ministry; and this is, To read and abridge, at their spare hours, every week, some of the best Practical Sermons they can meet with, in order to give them an early taste of Divinity; to form their style; improve their knowledge in such studies as are to be the business of their life; furnish them with proper expressions; and, above all, to fill their minds with saving truths.

The abridgment may be very short, and yet contain abundance of matter; such as, the manner of handling the subject; the way of reasoning; the most convincing arguments; the most moving exhortations, &c.

And this will be so far from making you lazy, that it will engage you to take pains, and to endeavour to collect, and suit all that you meet with to the necessities of the place and people to whom you shall be sent. For assure yourself, there are very few discourses that are nicely proper for any other place and circumstances than those for which they were composed.

By thus reading and abridging two Sermons every week, (which may be done at evenings before you go to bed, and you will not sleep the worse,) you will, in a few years, have such a fund of sound divinity, so fixed in your heart and memory, as that you will be able to speak and write upon any necessary subject; and in some good measure answer the character of the householder mentioned by our Saviour[p], *"which bringeth out of his treasure things new and old."*

And if you always set about this exercise

p Matt. xiii. 52.

with a short ejaculation, (which I cannot too often inculcate,) *that God would enlighten your mind with saving truth*, you will draw down God's blessing upon your labours, and you will be sure to fix upon such things as are *instructive*, rather than *curious*.

The Sermons I would recommend to you are such as you may borrow; (especially if you use books with care;) for I consider the length of your purse. Such are, Archbishop Sharp's, Bishop Bull's, Mr. Blair's Sermons on our Saviour's Sermon on the Mount, several of Bishop Hopkins's, or any other practical Sermons you can meet with:—I say practical; for if you will take my advice, you should not read any one book of controversy, until you shall be in full orders, except such only as are necessary to explain the Thirty-nine Articles of Religion. If you know the truth, you will easily see what is contrary to it, according to the old rule:—*Regula est regula recti et obliqui*.

Keep close to your studies; and believe it for a certain truth, that an habit of trifling, not resisted, will insensibly grow upon you; it will be as hard to be conquered, as any other vice whatever.

I doubt not but you will be strictly careful of your life and manners; what company you keep, &c. That you may give no offence, and that such as must hereafter sign your Testimonials may do it with pleasure, and with a good conscience.

I have this only further to advise you at present,—That you be very careful not to concern yourself in the unhappy misunderstandings which are now the curse of this once quiet nation; otherwise you will create yourself enemies; you will possess your mind, perhaps, with unjust prejudices; you will divert your thoughts from things of much greater concern to you; and, which is well to be considered, you will insensibly run into a crime, which for its commonness is scarce thought any,—*of speaking evil of the government, whether in Church or State;* which are both the ordinances of God, and not to be reviled, but at the peril of our souls.

y God direct and bless you, your inten-
your studies, and your affections, that
ay be esteemed both for your piety, and
ur endowments!

THOMAS SODOR AND MAN.

ATECHETICAL INSTRUCTION

FOR

CANDIDATES FOR HOLY ORDERS.

CATECHETICAL INSTRUCTION.

Q. WHAT is the end and design of the Christian Ministry?

A. To turn men from darkness to light, and from the power of Satan unto God; that they may obtain remission of sin, and be made eternally happy[r].

Q. By what name are the Ministers of Christ dignified in the Scriptures?

A. They are styled the *Ambassadors* of Christ, and *Stewards* of the Mysteries of God.

Q. Why are they styled Christ's Ambassadors?

A. Because they are sent by Christ to preach the Gospel.

[r] Acts xxvi. 18.

Q. What is meant by the word *Gospel?*

A. It signifies *good news,* or *good tidings of great joy,* as the Angel[s] expoundeth it.

Q. What are the good tidings which Christ, by these His Ambassadors, has sent to men?

A. The message is this:—That all men being sinners, and as such under the displeasure of their Maker, He is ready to be reconciled to them, on account of what His Son has done and suffered for them.

Q. How ought the Ministers of Christ to be qualified?

A. They ought to be regularly called and ordained. They ought to understand well the message which they are to bring from God to men. They are to have at heart the value of souls, which Christ hath purchased with His own blood. Their lives are to be without reproach, and their conduct such as becomes the Ministers of Jesus Christ. Lastly; They ought to have applied themselves to the study of the Holy Scriptures; in which their own

* Luke ii. 10.

duty, and the will of God, is contained, and His message to men.

Q. What is the duty and office of the Ministers of Christ?

A. Their duty is, To preach the Gospel;— to administer the means of grace and salvation; —to reprove and rebuke sinners;—to comfort the afflicted;—to endeavour to reduce those that are out of the way;—to pray daily for their people, and for themselves, that they may faithfully discharge the duties of their high calling.

Q. What especial motives have they to do this faithfully?

A. First; The reward promised by Christ, which is inexpressibly great, even *"a crown of glory that fadeth not away* [t].*"*

And secondly; The strict account they must give, and the punishment of their unfaithfulness. *If any man, for want of warning given him, perish, his blood will I require at the Watchman's hand* [u].

Q. When is a Minister of Christ regularly called to that office?

[t] 1 Pet. v. 4.   [u] Ezek. xxxiii. 6.

A. There is an outward and an inward call. Such as are called and ordained according to the laws of the Church where they are to serve. The *inward call* depends upon the motives and purposes which lead them to undertake the Ministry; which the learned Mr. Calvin sets down in these words:

"Arcana vocatio est cordis nostri testimonium, quod neque ambitione, neque avaritia, neque ulla alia cupiditate, sed sincero Dei timore, et ædificandæ Ecclesiæ studio, oblatum munus recipiamus[x]."

When Jesus Christ had called and ordained His Apostles, the charge He gave them was[y], " *That repentance and remission of sins should be preached in His Name unto all nations;*" namely, Repentance *on man's part*, and Forgiveness of Sins *on God's part*. Pursuant to this command, "*they went out and preached that men should repent[z].*"

Q. Why were they to begin their preaching with the subject of repentance?

[x] Instit. lib. iv. cap. 3.   [y] Luke xxiv. 47.
[z] Mark vi. 12.

A. Because all men being sinners, and as such under the displeasure of God, it was necessary they should repent, in order to obtain forgiveness from God, that they might be restored to His favour.

Q. How came all men to be sinners, and under the displeasure of their Maker?

A. Because of the sin and disobedience of our first parents.

Q. Were the parents of mankind created with such dispositions as did naturally lead them to disobey their Maker?

A. Very far from it!—They were created in the *image of God;* with a power of obeying any command which their Maker should think fit to give them for the trial of their obedience.

As Adam in Paradise had his trial; so have every one of his posterity a command, a duty, and a trial of their obedience.

Q. In what did the image of God consist?

A. That is best understood in our Lord Jesus Christ, *Who was the express image of God;* most holy, just, and good; in Whom the love, mercy, holiness, and goodness of the invisible God, was made known unto men. This was the image of God in which man was created.

Q. Did our first parents continue in that good estate?

A. No; they fell from it, and in a great measure lost that image and the favour of God, by disobeying His commands.

Q. How came our first parents to be guilty of so great a crime?

A. Through the temptation of the devil; who persuaded them not to give credit to their Maker, who had told them, that they should die if they disobeyed the command He had given them. Secondly, The devil assured them, that that command which God had given was not for their good; for that by eating of the forbidden fruit they would become as wise and good as God Himself. And giving credit to the devil, they disobeyed their Maker's command, and became slaves to that evil spirit.

And let it be observed, that this was the

same which provoked God to turn Satan himself, and his devils, out of Heaven;—disobedience to God, and affecting to be as His Maker.

Q. What followed upon this disobedience and transgression?

A. They forfeited that happiness which God had promised them; and Satan, having got thus far a power over them, would for ever have led them captive at his will, had not God, of His infinite mercy and goodness, found out a way to deliver them out of his power.

We see how afraid we should be of every sin, since our first parents suffered so much by it. Here the Ministers of Christ must begin, as ever they hope for success in their Ministry. Sinners must feel their danger before they will look out for or value a Saviour. The lame and the blind went to Christ, because they would be healed, &c.

Q. How did this sin of theirs affect their posterity?

A. The Scriptures tell us, that Adam begat

children "*in his own likeness,*" or image; that is, with such a corrupt and depraved nature as his was now become.

Q. Are then all men born in sin, and prone to evil, and as such under the displeasure of their Maker?

A. Most certainly so;—"*for all have sinned, and come short of the glory of God;*" that is, of that glorious happiness for which they were created. And we have mournful instances of this hereditary depravity before our eyes, in the pride, disobedience, hatred, malice, revenge, uncharitableness, lusts, uncleanness, injustice, and all manner of wickedness. These are the fruits of our depraved nature. This is called *original sin*, which every man born of Adam by *natural generation*, brings into the world with him.

Q. Of what use is the knowledge of this *original sin?*

A. The knowledge of our fall in Adam, and of our recovery in Christ, are the two fundamental principles of Christianity; and the order in which it is to be proposed and preached unto men. Here the Ministers of the Gospel must begin, as ever they hope for success:—For till sinners are sensible of their *guilt*, of their *slavery*, and *danger*, they will hardly be persuaded to look out for help; nor perceive the blessing of a Redeemer, till they know that they are in bondage, and under the tyranny of sin and Satan. In one word, till we are sensible that we want help, and that we cannot help ourselves, we shall never in good earnest flee to God, and beseech Him to help us.

Q. Hath not God given all men reason; and is not that sufficient to shew them their danger, and how to avoid it?

A. We see *that* in Adam, who had reason in perfection; and yet having free will, he acted against his reason, and sinned most grievously. He (as many of his posterity do) would depend upon himself, and his own reason, without believing and depending upon God; and we see what followed.

Q. What are the Ministers of Christ directed to do, in order to awaken sinners, and to convince them of the danger they are in, and to make them afraid for themselves?

A. They are to set before them the terrors of the Law; "*for by the Law is the knowledge of sin*[a];" that is, what sin deserves, and what will certainly follow, if sinners do not repent and turn to God, and bring forth fruits meet for repentance.

Q. What may be hoped will follow from setting before sinners the terrors of the Law?

A. When a sinner hears how the wrath of God is revealed from Heaven against all ungodliness and unrighteousness of men, if he be sincerely afraid for himself, God will open his eyes; so that he will perceive his misery and danger, and will not be easy till he knows WHAT HE MUST DO TO BE SAVED.

Q. What encouragement have sinners to hope that God will receive them into favour, accept of their repentance, and pardon their sins?

A. We have the surest proof of this, that the heart of a sinner can desire; since the Son

[a] Rom. iii. 20.

of God died for us, to assure us of the sincere love of His Father for His poor creatures, and that He will be thoroughly reconciled to them, if they will but be reconciled to the means which He has proposed to restore them to His favour.

Q. What way and means hath God appointed to mend the corruption of our nature, and to restore us to His favour?

A. The Christian religion is the way appointed by God to mend what is amiss in us; to restore us to His image and to His favour; and to fit us for Heaven and happiness.   In short, it is the only sure and merciful way to reclaim men from their sin;—to keep them from ruining themselves, and to make them partakers of the Divine nature.

Q. What is the end of religion?

A. It is to instruct and lead us in the way to be happy when we die, that God may be glorified in our salvation.

Q. What are the chief heads of the Christian religion?

A.   First. That " *God so loved the world*

*that He gave His only-begotten Son, that who-
soever believeth in Him, should not perish, but
have everlasting life* b."

Secondly. That this Son of God is "*the
Way, the Truth, and the Life* c;" that is, *He*
is the *Author* of the *way*, the *Teacher* of the
truth, and the *Giver* of *life*.

Thirdly. That " whosoever *believeth* in Him
shall receive remission of sins d;" and that He
is "the Author of salvation to all them that
obey Him e."

All which is contained in those comprehen-
sive words of the Apostle f, "Jesus Christ is
made unto us *Wisdom*, and *Righteousness*, and
Sanctification, and *Redemption*."

Q. What is the meaning of these words?

A. It is this:—That the world being ignorant of God, Jesus Christ became their *Wisdom*, by revealing to us the true God, and His
will; by bringing life and immortality to
light, through the Gospel.—That being sin-

---

b John iii. 16.   c John xiv. 6.
d Acts x. 43.   e Heb. v. 9.
f 1 Cor. i. 30.

ners, He became our *Righteousness*, by satisfying, in our nature, and in our stead, the justice of God, and procuring for us the forgiveness of sins ;—that by procuring for us the gifts of His Holy Spirit to purify our souls, He became our *Sanctification.*—And lastly ; the whole world being in bondage, and slaves to sin and Satan, and to the corruption of nature, Jesus Christ became our *Redeemer*, by paying the full price of our *redemption.*

Q. What is required on man's part, in order to be made partaker of these blessings ?

A. A *saving faith,* a *true repentance,* and a *sincere obedience.*

Q. What is a *saving faith ?*

A. It is the receiving and believing in Jesus Christ, as He is proposed to us in the Holy Scriptures.

Faith is a certain persuasion, and solid *trust,* in the goodness and mercy of God, obtained by Jesus Christ for the pardon of sin, and eternal life for all such as with sincere repentance, and sincere obedience, lay claim to those blessings.

Q. How is Jesus Christ proposed to us in the Holy Scriptures ?

A. As our P*rophet ;* as our P*riest ;* and as our *King.*

We are to believe Him to be a **Prophet,** and receive Him as sent from God, to declare God's will to men, and the way by which they must hope to be saved. We believe Him to be a **Priest,** Who offered Himself a *sacrifice,* to make our reconciliation with God; by virtue of which sacrifice, He maketh continual intercession for all such as repent and believe in Him. We believe Him to be our *King,* when we obey His laws, and suffer Him to reign over us.

Q. How may a Christian satisfy himself that he hath a true and saving faith ?

A. By such marks and fruits as these following, it will appear that we have a true and saving faith :

First. *If our faith purifies our hearts ;* that is, if there is a change made in our hearts for the better ; if the desire of our hearts is to please and glorify God.

Secondly. If our faith *worketh by love ;*

that is, if the love of God for us obliges us to love our neighbour.

Thirdly. If our faith shews itself in our life and actions, enabling us to overcome the world, the flesh, and the devil. It is then *a true and saving faith*[g].

Q. Thus far of the first thing required of a Christian—*a saving faith.* What is a *true and saving repentance ?*

A. A true and saving repentance consists in such a sincere sorrow as makes a sinner to hate and forsake every sin whatever, and this out of a sense, and shame, and concern for having offended the best of Fathers, and the

[g] MAXIMS *of the Christian Faith, or* RELIGION.—That there is one *God*, the Maker of all things ; one *Redeemer*, the Lord Jesus Christ ; and one *Holy Ghost*, the Sanctifier of the chosen people of God. That God would have all men to be saved ;— that therefore He sent His own Son from Heaven, to shew men the way of salvation ;—that this His Son has reconciled us to God ;—that He is our Advocate with God, to obtain for us all ne- cessary assistance and blessings.—That God will give His *Holy Spirit* to such as pray for Him ;—that He has given the Holy Scriptures to be the rule of our faith, of our lives and actions ;— that He will call all men to an account ;—that such as have lived according to His Word and Will, shall by Him be made happy for ever ; and that such as have done evil, have led evil lives, and have not repented, shall have their portion with devils.

most gracious God[h]; such a *sorrow* as doth melt and soften a heart that was hardened by sin ; and, lastly, such a *sorrow* as will oblige a sinner to submit to any means of grace, how bitter soever, that is required or necessary to root sin out of his soul, and to repair the dishonour done to God, by disobeying His commands, and breaking His laws.

Repentance, which is so much insisted on as the great condition of the Gospel, is expressed by other words, signifying *the great change* made or to be made by repentance ; such as, *conversion; regeneration,* a *being born again* of *God*—made *a new creature; self-denial, mortification, &c.*

Q. Is there danger of being mistaken in this important duty ?

[h] The most effectual means of our recovery from what we are fallen, consists in a firm faith in the power and love of God, to root out whatever is amiss in us, and displeasing to Him.— Secondly. In praying earnestly to God, to make us sensible of our faults, and to avoid, and resist, and overcome, and root all evil out of our souls.—And thirdly. A sincere care and endeavour, that on our part we do what is in our power to avoid sin, and to conquer it.—Dr. MOORE.

A. Very great danger!—Such as place repentance only in making confession of their sins, without amendment of life;—such as depend upon good purposes, or upon a death-bed repentance, or in forsaking sin, without a change of heart;—or finally, such as place all their hopes of pardon in their repentance, and not in the merits and blood of Jesus Christ, by which alone all our sins will be forgiven.

Q. The next thing necessary to salvation is *new obedience.* What is meant by *new obedience?*

A. When once a man is in Christ, that is, a Christian, he is no longer at his own disposal, to live as he pleases;—he has rules to live by, and by which he must be judged at the last day. In order to this obedience, he will be obliged to *deny himself* all ungodliness and worldly lusts; that he may live soberly, righteously, and godly, in this present evil world. His will must become subject to the will and law of God; his conversation must be such as becomes the Gospel of Christ. In short, he must become a *new man*, a *new crea-ture*, walk in *newness of life*, and continue patient in well-doing; putting off daily the old man, as children of Adam, who by his dis-obedience lost all right to the tree of life, that is, to eternal life and happiness; to regain which right, a Christian must put on the new man, made after the image of God, as ever he hopes for Heaven.

Q. Doth God require a *perfect obedience* to His commands?

A. God knoweth our weakness and our infirmities; as a Father, He will accept of a dutiful and sincere obedience, though mixed with many imperfections; provided we strive against such failings, pray for a greater mea-sure of obedience and holiness, and labour after it.

Q. Are not Christians too apt to value themselves for their obedience and good works, and think they merit by them?

A. Many are apt to do so; but it is very wrong:—For let a man have been never so exact in his obedience, and done never so many good works, he has but done his duty, and has nothing to boast of, or claim any thing by his merit.   In short, neither our *faith*, nor our *repentance*, nor our *obedience*, though never so perfect, can merit either our *justification*, our *pardon*, or *reward*.   These are the free gift of God, purchased for all such as *believe* and *repent* and become obedient by the merits of Jesus Christ, and through faith in His blood.

Q. What is *justification?*

A. It is to absolve a person from the guilt of sin, and free him from that sentence of condemnation passed upon mankind in Adam, and from God's displeasure for our sins.

When a person, by the Spirit of God, is convinced of his guilt and danger, and repents and flies to God for help; when God, passing by the punishment which such a sinner has deserved, pardons him, and admits him into favour, and into a state of salvation, *such a person is said to be justified.*   Now all this is owing to the mere free grace, and mercy, and goodness of God; on account of what Jesus

Christ hath done and suffered for us, not for any thing that any man has done, or can do.

Q. The Law, the moral Law, our Lord assures us, shall last and be in force as long as the world lasts. What are *moral Laws,* or commands?

A. They are concerning such things as are in themselves good or evil, though they had never been commanded or forbidden; they are really such as the conscience of every man cannot but assent to, when he hears them. But forasmuch as man, after the fall, became unwilling to consult his own reason and conscience, God ordered these laws to be engraved upon tables of stone, that all might read them, and be without excuse if they transgressed them. These are called the *Ten Commandments;* and contain the duties we owe to God, to our neighbour, and to ourselves.

Q. Hath not our Saviour Christ summed up these Ten Commandments in fewer words?

A. He hath done so in these words: " *Thou shalt love the Lord thy God with all thy heart, and with all thy soul; with all thy mind,*

and with all thy strength."   This is the *first*
commandment; and the second is like, namely
this,—" *Thou shalt love thy neighbour as thy-*
self."

Q. When may we be said thus to love
God?

A. When we sincerely endeavour to keep
His commandments, and do such things as we
know will please Him i.

Q. When may we be said to love our neighbour as ourselves?

A. When we love others, (for all are our
neighbours,) as men fearing God love themselves; or, as our Lord explains it, " *As ye*
would that men should do unto you, do ye
also to them likewise."   And Christians have
a very particular reason and motive given
them for loving their neighbour, *Because*
Jesus Christ " *loved us,*" *and* " *laid down His life*
for us k;" and because they are related to Jesus
Christ, (He having taken our nature upon
Him,) Who is therefore greatly concerned for
the good of every man living, and laid down

i 1 John iii. 22.   k 1 John iii. 16.

His life for them, though they were His enemies.

Q. Are there not other duties and commands which Christ hath required of us as Christians?

A. There are, and especially those of *self-denial* and *watchfulness,* which comprehend the rest; and are absolutely necessary to our salvation, and suited to all our ailments.

Q. Why hath Christ commanded self-denial?

A. Not because He can command what He pleaseth; but because the corruption of our nature requires it, and that we should be hindered from every thing that would ruin us.

For instance; we are really blind with regard to what would hurt and ruin us; we are therefore commanded *to deny our own wisdom.*—Intemperance would injure both our souls and bodies; we are therefore commanded *to deny our appetites.*—We are required to keep a *strict watch over our hearts,* because from thence proceed a thousand evils.—And because our eternal happiness depends upon our loving God with all our heart, we are *forbid to set our hearts upon the world.*—And because, as sinners, suffering is our due, we are forbid all repining when God afflicts us.—And because our bodies have a great influence over our souls, we are not only commanded to *be always temperate*, but to *fast* sometimes, and to deny ourselves the pleasure of indulging the appetite.

These, and other such duties, are commanded purely because they are necessary, either to cure our corruption, or to qualify us to receive the grace of God ; or to hinder us from grieving His Holy Spirit, and forcing Him to forsake us.

Q. Are we able of ourselves to do these things, and to keep the commands of God?

A. We are not.—Our sufficiency must be from God ; Who has promised to help us to overcome all the difficulties we can possibly meet with in the way of our duty[c].

Q. What do the Holy Scriptures direct us to, in order to obtain the grace and help of God ?

A. To earnest prayer. For so we are as-

c Luke xi. 9.

sured, that God will give the Holy Spirit and all other blessings to them that ask Him, and that make use of the other *means* of grace and salvation which God has appointed.

Q. What are the means of grace?

A. They are chiefly these :—*Prayer*, the *Holy Scriptures*, and the *Sacraments*.

Q. What is *Prayer?*

A. Prayer is the making our wants known unto God, and begging Him to give us such things, as in His wisdom and goodness shall seem best for us, and for His glory.

Q. Doth not God know all our wants?

A. Most certainly He doth so ; even better than we ourselves do. But He would have us to know and to remember, that we depend upon Him for life, and breath, and all things ; and that we may receive His favours with thanksgiving.

Q. What encouragement have we to believe that God will grant our requests?

A. Even the greatest that our hearts can desire. "*Verily,* (saith His only Son) *whatsoever ye shall ask the Father in My Name, He* *will give it you*d." These being the conditions of being heard :—that we ask such things as are agreeable to God's will; and in the Name, and for the sake of Jesus Christ.

Q. How may we be sure to ask nothing but what is agreeable to His will?

A. He Himself has given us a short form of prayer, not only to direct us what to pray for, but also as a form of prayer; that none may want words, by which to lay before God the desires of their hearts.

Q. With what disposition should we pray, so as that we may be accepted of God?

A. That we pray with *humility ;*—for " *God resisteth the proud, but giveth grace unto the humble*k." Secondly. With *submission:*—"*Not my will, but Thine be done.*" Thirdly. With a *forgiving temper* towards all that have injured us. Fourthly. With a full purpose of leading a godly, righteous, and sober life. `

Q. Are not *praise* and *thanksgiving* a part of that service which we owe to God?

A. They are certainly so. And it is much

k John xvi. 23.   l James iv. 6.

to be feared, that Christians do too often put a stop to, and deprive themselves of many blessings, by their ingratitude, and for want of taking notice of the favours and mercies they every day receive, and giving thanks to God for them.

Q. How may the *Lord's Prayer* become a pattern, and direct us how, and what, to pray for?

A. As followeth :

OUR FATHER, WHICH ART IN HEAVEN.

By this we are directed to apply to God, the Lord of Heaven and earth, with reverence and godly fear :—and at the same time with confidence of being heard; for " *as a father pitieth his own children, so is the Lord merciful to them that fear Him*[1]."

HALLOWED BE THY NAME.

This teacheth us, that the glory of God ought to be the first in our thoughts and desires : He being worthy to receive honour, and glory,

[1] Psalm ciii. 13.

and power; for He hath created all things, and by His will they all subsist[e].

THY KINGDOM COME.

By this we are directed both to pray, and to endeavour, that the Gospel of Christ may be propagated in all the world; that the kingdoms of the world (all that are now the slaves of Satan) may become the Kingdom of the *L*ord, and of His Christ, that He may reign for ever and ever [f].

THY WILL BE DONE IN EARTH, AS IT IS IN HEAVEN.

Which is designed to teach us, to have the highest regard for the will and providence of God in the government of the world;—to resign our will and desires to Him, Who only knows what is best for us;—never to dispute or question the will and orders of One, Who is infinitely *wise*, and *holy*, and *good;* but to sub-

---

[e] Rev. iv. 11.   [f] Rev. xi. 15.

mit, and with pleasure close with it, as the best that can be ordered for ourselves or others.

GIVE US THIS DAY OUR DAILY BREAD.

To put us in mind, that it is God that giveth food unto all flesh ;—that our Heavenly Father knoweth what things we have need of ;—and that where He gives abundance, He expects that we should impart to the rest of His children that are in want, of what He has given us more than our daily bread.

But above all things, we are hereby directed to pray *for the Bread that nourisheth to eternal life.*

FORGIVE US OUR TRESPASSES, AS WE FORGIVE THEM THAT TRESPASS AGAINST US.

Here is matter of direction and comfort for sinners !—If we find our hearts disposed to forgive others, He, Who put this grace into our hearts, assures us by this, that our sins shall be forgiven. So that our first petition should always be, That the good Spirit of God may give us a forgiving temper.

AND LEAD US NOT INTO TEMPTATION, BUT DELIVER US FROM EVIL.

In this petition we are directed, never to trust in our own strength ; for it is God only, Who can deliver us from *evil;* from the *evil one;* from an *evil world;* and from our own evil and corrupt hearts.   He only can enable us to escape the corruption that is in the world through lust, that we may be partakers of the Divine nature.   He only, in all our saving trials and temptations, can enable us to overcome to His glory.

FOR THINE IS THE KINGDOM, AND THE POWER AND THE GLORY, FOR EVER AND EVER. AMEN.

Here we are directed to acknowledge God in every thing we do, or pray for.   As the only sure foundation of all our hopes, to Him we pray ; on Him we depend ; to Him we stand obliged ; to Him we give thanks:—For He only hath *power*, and ought to have the glory of all the blessings we enjoy, or hope for, in this world, or in the world to come. *Amen.*

Q. The WORD OF GOD is another *means of grace.*—How doth it become such ?

A. As it is intended, and sufficient, through the grace of God, to make men wise unto salvation : " *being profitable for doctrine, for reproof, for instruction in the way of righteousness ;*" and, as such, is the great instrument of men's conversion.

Q. How doth it become instrumental to conversion ?

A. By hearing it read or preached ; by receiving it into an honest and good heart,—an heart sincerely disposed to receive the truth ; with prayer to God for grace to practise it in our lives.

Q. Hath the Word of God this effect upon all that read or hear it ?

A. No ; God knows it has not. Some

despise it, and will not read it;—and by many, the cares and pleasures of this life, and the deceitfulness of riches, and the lusts of other _things, hinder the word, so that it bringeth no fruit to perfection.

Q. How are the SACRAMENTS means of grace and salvation ?

A. As they are means appointed by Jesus Christ.   *F*irst; For admitting us into His Family, which is His Church, out of which there is no appointed means of salvation: and, secondly; By making us worthy members of His Church and Family, by engaging us to lead a new and Christian life.

Q. Which are the Sacraments of the Christian religion ?

A. They are two only ; namely, *Baptism,* and the *Lord's Supper.*

Q. What is *Baptism ?*

A. Baptism is a solemn dedication of a person to *God,* the Creator ; to *Jesus Christ,* the Redeemer of the world ; and to the *Holy Ghost,* the Sanctifier of all such as shall be saved.

Q. How is this solemn dedication performed?

A. By washing the person with water, in the Name of the *Father, Son,* and *Holy Ghost.*

Q. What is signified by this outward sign?

A. That such a person is washed from his former pollutions, and restored to the favour of God.

Q. What other names are given in the Gospel to this Sacrament?

A. It is called *Regeneration,* or the *New Birth,* or being made a *new creature,* &c., or *being born again* g.

Q. Why is it so called?

A. Because, as we did receive a natural life from our parents, as descendants of Adam, subject to sin and misery; so by Baptism, we receive the Holy Spirit for a principle of a new and Christian life, and as truly as we did

---

g *Regeneration,* or *New Birth,* is that spiritual change that is wrought by the Holy Spirit upon any person in the use of Baptism; whereby he is translated out of his natural state as a descendant of Adam, to a spiritual state in Christ; that is, to a state of salvation; in which, if it is not his own fault, he will be saved.

receive a natural life from our parents :—And being thus engrafted into Christ, or His Church, we receive grace and a new life from Christ, as really as a branch receives life and nourishment from the good tree in which it is grafted. This is called the *preventing grace* of God, or His *free gift;* because we have done nothing to deserve such a favour.

Q. What doth this free grace of God oblige Christians to ?

A. To honour God, their Maker, their Redeemer, and Sanctifier, by an holy and Christian life ; and especially, not to grieve the Holy Spirit, by which they have been sanctified, and by which alone they can be secured from falling into a state of heathenism, and into the power of sin and Satan.

Q. What must they do, who have been so unhappy as to have grieved that Holy Spirit; and though they have been baptized, *yet are not renewed by the Holy Ghost?*

A. Such unhappy people (and too great, God knows, is their number) have no other choice, but *repentance* or *damnation.* So the

Apostle tells Simon Magus, who had received the washing of regeneration, and so was entitled to pardon upon his repentance; which the Apostle exhorted him to, to prevent his eternal ruin.

Q. What is the other Sacrament, or means of grace, which is called the *Lord's Supper?*

A. It is an Ordinance appointed by Christ, by which the worthy receiver is made partaker of all the graces and blessings which Jesus Christ has purchased by His death.

Q. What are the graces and blessings which Jesus Christ by His death hath purchased for such Christians as are worthy partakers of this Sacrament ?

A. The pardon of our sins ;—new degrees and supplies of grace and strength to do our duty; which, if we continue to do,—eternal happiness when we die ;—which we may expect as surely as we do expect health and strength from the daily food we eat.

Q. Who are worthy receivers of this Sacrament ?

A. Such as seriously consider the state of

their souls ;—whether they have sincerely repented of their sins ;—whether they as sincerely resolve to lead a Christian life, renew-
ing their vow made in Baptism ;—whether
they have a lively faith in God's mercy
through Christ;—and are in love and charity
with their neighbours ; that is, with all the
world.

Q. What is signified by the bread and wine
made use of in this Sacrament ?

A. After the bread and wine are conse-
crated, by giving of thanks and prayer, the
bread is broken, to put us in mind of Christ's
sufferings ;—and the wine is poured out, as
the Blood of Christ was, for the sins of the
world.

Q. What ought to be a serious Christian's
thoughts upon this ?

A. Every understanding Christian will
conclude :

*F*irst. That all sin must be hateful to God,
since it required such a sacrifice,—the life
and blood of Jesus Christ.—If any thing will
touch our hearts with godly sorrow, and a re-

pentance not to be repented of, this, through the grace of God, will do it.

Secondly. This will oblige us to lead a Christian life ; since nothing can be more just and reasonable, than to consecrate a life to Him, which He has redeemed with His most precious Blood.

Thirdly. This Sacrament ought to be a powerful motive to oblige Christians to love one another ; since we are one body under one Head, which is Christ ; and therefore ought to have one heart. The design of this Ordinance is to unite us in love and charity. We worship the same God and Saviour ; we hope for the same salvation ; we eat at one and the same Table ; we eat the same Bread which came down from Heaven ; and we ought to live by one and the same Spirit.

Lastly. This Sacrament is a representation of the greatest love of Christ ; a love for sinners ; a love for enemies ; a love expressed in laying down His life for us. This sure should oblige us to love one another, not in word only, but in deed and truth.

Q. Who are appointed to administer to Christians these means of grace and salvation?

A. They are such as are regularly ordained and appointed for that office; spiritual Governors, Pastors, and Teachers; who watch for the souls of their flock; whose prayers are heard, in a more especial manner, for those over whom the Holy Ghost hath made them overseers; who receive Christians into the Church, out of which there is no appointed means of salvation. These, and many other things, are their duty and their charge.

Q. What is the duty of Christians to these Ministers of Christ?

A. To honour them for their work's sake, and for their Master Christ's sake; and to obey their godly admonitions.

EXCOMMUNICATION.

EXCOMMUNICATION.

My Brethren, and all good Christians here met together,

WE are met upon a very *unusual* and *mournful* occasion.

We have hitherto (blessed be God!) preserved, in some good measure, the ancient discipline of the Church; and notorious sinners have been prevailed upon to take shame to themselves in a public confession of their offences; and to desire the prayers of the Church for the grace that is necessary for a *true conversion.*

I am sorry to tell you, that there is a person now under the censures of the Church, who utterly refuseth to submit to this wholesome discipline; being more concerned for the shame that attends its censures, than *he* is for *his* salvation.

We have laid before you *his* crimes; and the Christian methods which have been made use of to bring *him* to a sense of *his* guilt and danger, and to oblige *him* to make what satisfaction *he* can for the scandal *he* hath given.

You will see how very long we have waited in hopes of bringing *him* to submit to the discipline of the Church; until at last our discipline begins to be slighted, as too weak for such offenders.

However, it ought not to repent us that we have waited with patience; when we consider with what mighty patience God Himself waiteth to be gracious; and that the sentence of Excommunication was never, in the primitive Church, executed hastily, nor until all other probable ways had been made use of *without effect.*

Now, this being the last remedy which the Church can make use of for awakening obstinate offenders, the whole Church ought to be satisfied upon what grounds, and by what authority, we pronounce this sentence; and what will be the effects of such a sentence, when passed according to the will and appointment of Jesus Christ.

The Holy Scriptures tell us, that our Lord Jesus Christ, Who came to seek and to save His lost creatu es, has appointed divers Ordinances for the conversion and salvation of men.

For instance :—He has appointed *Preaching*, to draw men to Him; He has appointed the Sacrament of *Baptism*, by which we are admitted into His Household the Church ; and that of the *Lord's Supper*, as a pledge of His love, and of our communion with Him. And lastly; He hath ordained *godly discipline*, that such who do not live as becomes their Christian profession, may be ´reproved, corrected, and amended; or else cast out of His Church.

And all these Ordinances are committed unto His Ministers, who are also called His *Stewards;* because to them He has committed the keys of His House and Kingdom, that is, the Church; that they may admit such as are worthy, and that they may shut out such as behave themselves disorderly in His family.

Jesus Christ, I say, committed this power to His Apostles, and they to their successors; with this assurance from His own mouth, "*He that heareth you, heareth Me; and he that despiseth you, despiseth Me, and Him that sent Me*[h]."

So that you see, whoever makes a jest of Church discipline, makes a jest of an ordinance of God; and a man may as well despise the whole Christian religion, as *this* power, which is as much the ordinance of Jesus Christ, as preaching, or the use of the Sacraments.

The most unlearned Christian will understand this: When he is asked, for what end he was baptized? he will answer, That he might thereby be made *a member of Christ, a child of God, and an inheritor of the kingdom of Heaven.*

But why does he believe that Baptism does

[h] Luke x. 16.

give him a right to these blessings? Why; Because Jesus Christ gave power to His Ministers to baptize all nations; that such as are baptized into Christ, have put on Christ; that is, are members of Christ's Body, which is His Church.

Now, will not our Lord Christ, Who has promised to own you for His children when His Ministers have admitted you into His Church by Baptism; will not He also disown you, when the same Ministers, *acting in His name*, shall, by the same power of the keys, shut you out of His Church?

For if you believe that they receive you into Christ's Church by *Baptism*, you must believe that they shut you out as effectually by *Excommunication.*

In short; every Christian, when he is baptized, is admitted into the Church upon a most solemn promise to live as a Christian ought to do; if he does not do so, those very Ministers who admitted him are bound to *exhort*, to *rebuke*, and to *censure* him; and if these methods will not do, to *excommunicate him;*

that is, to cut him off from the body of Christ, and from God's favour and mercy. Not that he may be lost for ever, but that he may see his sad condition, and repent, and be saved.

The form of Excommunication made use of by the Apostles of our Lord, was, *by delivering offenders to Satan.* Now, because this is laughed at by profane people, who do not know the Scriptures, I will shew you what that means. The Spirit and Word of God has told us, that the devil has a kingdom and subjects, over whom *he* reigns; that is, *over the children of disobedience.*

That Jesus Christ has also *His* kingdom and subjects; and when the Apostles gained over any of the subjects of Satan unto Christ, they are said *"to turn them from darkness to light, and from the power of Satan unto God*₁*."*

Now, when any of Christ's subjects become rebellious, and refuse to be governed by the laws of the Gospel, His Ministers are bound to admonish them of their sin, and of their danger; and if they refuse to obey their

₁ Acts xxvi. 18.

godly admonitions, then to turn them out of that society of which Christ is the Head; and, consequently, *such persons* fall under the power of Satan again, who useth his subjects like slaves. And God permits him to do so, that sinners, if they are not utterly lost, may with the prodigal, when he was forced to herd with swine, see the state they are fallen from, and repent, and desire to get out of the snare and power of the devil, and be restored to the favour of God.

So that Excommunication is made use of, *not as a punishment only*, but as *a remedy;* that sinners seeing the evil state they are in, being deprived of all hopes of salvation while they are out of the Church, may desire to be restored to God's grace, from which they are fallen, that they may work out their salvation with more fear for the time to come.

But here I must take notice of one thing which often hinders the discipline of the Church from having this good effect upon sinners. They are apt to say, *If I am shut out of this Church, I can go to another.* Why;

has Christ more Churches than one? *"Is
Christ divided*k*?"* saith the Apostle. Do not all
Christians profess to believe one *Holy Apostolic*
Church? And is not this Church a member of
that holy Church? And have not the Ministers of Christ *here* the same authority from
their Lord and Prince, as any other Christian
Bishop; namely, the authority of *binding* and
loosing? And will not our sentence, when we
proceed according to the rules which Christ
hath given us, be confirmed in Heaven? If so,
what advantage will a sinner get by going to
another society, if after all Jesus Christ shall
confirm the sentence of his former Pastor; and,
for want of being reconciled by Him, shall
shut him out of Heaven?

It is true, our Lord hath not given us any
power to compel men *by outward force,* either
to come into, or to continue in His Church;
but will people for this reason despise the
power which Christ has given us? They will
hardly do so, if they know what St. Paul hath
said upon this[1]: "The weapons we use (saith

k 1 Cor. i. 13.   1 2 Cor. x. 4.

he) are not carnal, *but mighty through God;*"
that is, God can humble the stoutest sinner,
and make the power of His Ministers effectual,
when they use their power for His glory, and
according to His will.

You see, good Christians, that we take upon
us no authority but what Christ has given
us; what His Apostles exercised; and what
we are bound by our most *solemn vows* to
exercise.

Every Bishop, for instance, at his Consecra-
tion, solemnly promises, *that he will correct
and punish disobedient and criminous persons
within his Diocese, according to such authority
as he has by God's word.* What authority he
has by God's word, you have already heard.
And all serious Christians must acknowledge,
that we should become adversaries to ourselves,
to our Church, and to our country, if we
should suffer Church discipline to fall into
decay, while we are warranted and bound, both
by the laws of God, and of this land, to exercise it; especially when vices of this kind
begin to grow upon us.

Only let us take care that we use *this autho-rity*, as the Apostle directs, *"for edification, and not for destruction*ᵐ."

And if we must be forced to shut this un-happy person out of the Church, let it be with the same compassion and reluctancy that a father turns his rebellious child out of his house; not with a design that he should starve and be lost for ever; but that, being made sensible of the misery of being out of his father's house, he may more earnestly desire to return and be received into favour; and be-come a more dutiful child for the time to come.

God has infinite expedients to bring back sinners that are gone away from Him. We know how the prodigal son was brought to a sense of his condition by the miseries he met with when he was from under his father's care: how David's eyes were opened by a parable: how Manasseh became an instance of repent-ance when in bonds. And we should not despair, but be confident rather, that God will bless His own institutions in the hands of us

ᵐ 2 Cor. xiii. 10.

His Ministers, for the good of all such persons
as draw these censures upon themselves. And
it will be far from being severity to them, if
by these means they may be brought to a sense
of their evil condition, *and their souls "be saved
in the day of the Lord Jesus[n]."*

This is the design of Church censures ; and
that they may have this good effect, the
Apostle has given directions to all Christians
not to accompany with such, that they may
be ashamed[o]. And our holy Church in her
Articles, as you will find it in the thirty-third
Article of the Church of England, has declared
in these words :—*That person which by open
denunciation of the Church is rightly cut off
from the unity of the Church, and excommunicated, ought to be taken of the whole multitude
of the faithful, as an heathen and publican,
until he be openly reconciled by penance, and
received into the Church by a judge that hath
authority thereunto.*

Pursuant to which Article, the Church in
the eighty-fifth Canon appoints, *that all persons*

1 Cor. v. 5. 1 Cor. v. 11.

excommunicated, and so denounced, be kept out of the Church by the Churchwardens.

And in the sixty-fifth Canon directs, *That all such as stand lawfully excommunicated, shall every six months be openly denounced and declared excommunicate; that others may be thereby admonished to refrain their company and society, &c.*

As for any temporal penalties or incapacities which an excommunicate person may be exposed to; these do not properly belong to the Church; they are no part of our sentence; they are altogether in the hands of the civil Magistrate. Our sentence is purely spiritual; it is the sentence of Jesus Christ, and only concerns the good of the souls of those *He* has committed to our care. It is part of that Ministry which we received by the imposition of hands, and which we most humbly pray God to enable us to exercise, *to His glory*, to the putting a stop to the growing vices of the age, and to the edification of the Church of Christ, which He hath purchased with His Blood. *Amen.*

¶ *THE SENTENCE.*

I⊤ is with great reluctancy, (God is our witness,) and after many prayers to God for their conversion, that we proceed to this *last remedy* which Christ has appointed for the conversion of sinners.

But we hope you are not shut out, that you may ever remain out of the Church; but that you may become sensible of your errors, and return with more zeal to your Heavenly Father.

In the mean time, we must do our duty, and leave the event to God.

I⋉ the Name of Jesus Christ, and by the authority which we have received from Him, we separate you from the Communion of the Church, which He has purchased with His Blood, and which is the society of all faithful people; and you are no longer a member of His Body, or of His Kingdom, until you be openly reconciled by penance, and received into the Church by a judge that hath authority so to do.

¶ *When Persons Excommunicated are received back
into the Church.*

I, AN unworthy Minister of Jesus Christ, by
the same authority and power, even that of
our Lord Jesus Christ, by which for thy
obstinacy and other crimes, thou hast been
excluded from the Communion of Christ's
holy Church: by the same power, I do now
release thee from that bond of Excommunication, according to the confession now made
by thee before God and this Church; and do
restore thee again unto the Communion of
the Church of Christ; beseeching the Almighty to give thee His grace, that thou
mayest continue a worthy member of the same
unto thy life's end, through Jesus Christ our
Lord. *Amen.*

A

FORM

OF

RECEIVING PENITENTS.

To be duly and devoutly observed in all Churches and Chapels
within the Diocese of Man.

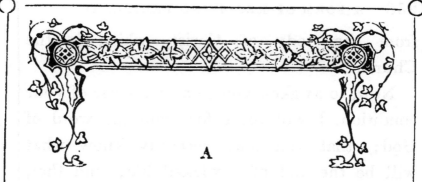

A

FORM OF RECEIVING PENITENTS.

¶ *After Morning Prayers, the person who is censured to Penance, standing in the accustomed place and habit, the Minister shall exhort him as follows:*

BROTHER,

THE Church being a society of persons professing to live in the fear of God, and expecting the judgments of God to fall upon them, if His laws are broken without calling the offenders to account; it is reasonable that every member of this society, who has been guilty o. any scandalous offence, should either openly confess *his* sins, and promise reformation for the time to come; or else should be cut off from the body of Christ, which is the Church.

Now, to awaken you to a true sense of your condition, I will set before you the word of God; that you may certainly know what will be the end of a wicked life; and that, knowing the terror of the Lord, you may speedily turn unto Him, and make your peace.

Hear then what the Apostle St. Paul saith of great offenders:

"Be not deceived: neither fornicators, nor adulterers, nor effeminate, nor thieves, nor covetous, nor drunkards, nor revilers, nor extortioners, shall inherit the kingdom of God P."

Hear also what the same Apostle saith:

"Now the works of the flesh are these; Adultery, fornication, uncleanness, lasciviousness, witchcraft, hatred, variance, emulations, wrath, strife, seditions, heresies, envyings, murders, drunkenness, revellings, and such like: of the which I tell you before, as I have

P 1 Cor. vi. 9.

also told you in time past, that they which do such things shall not inherit the Kingdom of Heaven[m]."

" It is a fearful thing to fall into the hands of the living God[n], Who can destroy both body and soul in hell[o]; where the worm dieth not, and the fire is not quenched[p]."

These being the very words of God, you will do well to consider into what a condition you have brought yourself.   And indeed, the only comfort you have is this, that you are yet alive, and that the day of grace and repentance is yet afforded you.   Which that you make use of, I must also let you know, what God has declared concerning such as repent and turn unto God, and bring forth fruits meet for repentance :—

" To the Lord our God belong mercies and forgivenesses, though we have rebelled against Him[q]."

" If we confess our sins, He is faithful and just to forgive us our sins[r]."

[m] Gal. v. 19—21.   [n] Heb. x. 31.   [o] Matt. x. 28.
[p] Mark ix. 44.   [q] Dan. ix. 9.   [r] 1 John i. 9.

And our blessed Saviour, to shew us what great compassion God has for him that has gone astray, and returns to his duty; He represents Him as a man, who, having found his lost sheep, takes it upon his shoulders, rejoicing.

And in another parable, to make us understand the love of God for penitent sinners, He shews us how we may hope to be received, even as a compassionate father received his prodigal son, when once he became humble and sensible of his faults; he embraced him, he clothed him, he rejoiced with his whole family. And such joy there is amongst the Angels of God, when a sinner repenteth [s].

Such great encouragement you have to return to God. But then, you must do it sincerely; you must not only appear outwardly a penitent, but with a true penitent heart come before God and His Church. Which if you do, you will not look upon this as a punishment inflicted upon you by the Church, but as a wholesome medicine administered for the

[s] Luke xv.

good of your precious soul. Without which, you might have gone on, adding sin to sin, until there had been no more space for repentance.

You will suffer yourself to be admonished; acknowledge your offence; and give glory to God, in owning His power to punish you in the next life, though you should escape in this.

You will testify to others, that it is indeed an evil thing and bitter to forsake the Lord. And owning this so publicly, you will be ashamed to return to the sins you have repented of.

Then we shall all pray to God that He would, for Christ's sake, accept of your repentance; that He would enable you to live for the time to come in obedience to the laws of Jesus Christ, that your soul may be saved at the Day of Judgment.

These are the wholesome ends the Church proposes in her censures; following herein the Apostle's direction[t], *" in meekness instructing*

[t] 2 Tim. ii. 25, 26.

those that oppose themselves;"—"that they may recover themselves out of the snare of the devil, who are taken captive by him at his will."

Therefore (*dear brother*) consider that you are in the presence of God, the Searcher of hearts. You may indeed deceive this congregation with a feigned repentance, but you cannot deceive Him that made you; Who, if you dissemble in this matter, will shut you out of Heaven, though you continue a visible member of His Church here.

But that we may take all due caution, I must, in the name of this congregation, ask you these questions:—

Are you from your heart sorry for the sin you have committed?

I am.

Will you be more careful for the time to come; and, by God's help, avoid all temptations to it?

I will.

Will you constantly pray to God to assist you to do so?

I will.

Do you desire the forgiveness of all good Christians whom you may have offended?

I do.

And do you desire that others, seeing your sorrow, may beware of falling into any grievous sin?

I do desire it.

Will you take patiently the admonition of such as after a Christian manner shall advise you, if they shall see you forget yourself and the promises you have now made?

I will.

¶ *Then shall the Minister say,*

May the gracious God give you repentance to life eternal; receive you into His favour; continue you a true member of the Church of Christ; and bring you unto His everlasting Kingdom, through the same Jesus Christ our *Lord. Amen.*

¶ *After which he shall speak to the Congregation, as follows:*

Seeing now, dearly beloved brethren, that this person is moved by the good Spirit of God to confess *his* sins, and to be afflicted for them; Let us, that we may mourn with *him* as becomes good Christians, consider that we are all subject to sin, and to death eternal.

That there is nothing so vile and wicked which we should not run into, did not the grace of God prevent us.

That therefore we have nothing to value ourselves for above others, but what the good Spirit of God has given us.

"Let him then," as the Apostle advises, "that thinketh he standeth, take heed lest he fall[u]."

Let us ever remember the words of Christ, "*Watch and pray, that ye enter not into temptation;*" because our adversary the devil, as a roaring lion, walketh continually about, seeking whom he may devour.

* 1 Cor. x. 12.

Let us learn never to be ashamed to acknowledge our sins, but let us confess and forsake them, that we may find mercy.   For it is far better to suffer shame here, than the wrath of God hereafter.

In a word; let us all with penitent hearts call our sins to remembrance, and judge ourselves, though we are not censured by the Church.   Let us confess our sins unto God, Who is most willing to pardon us, if we turn unto Him with all our hearts, stedfastly purposing to lead a new life.   Which God grant we may all do, for Jesus Christ His sake. *Amen.*

¶ *Then shall be said* distinctly *the fifty-first Psalm, together with the Prayers appointed* (in the Commination Office) *for Ash-Wednesday.*

My Brethren,

In the Form for receiving Penitents, there ought to have been a Prayer for persons performing penance, who are not yet to be received into the peace of the Church; I have therefore sent the enclosed Form of Prayer, which I desire you to take a copy of, to be constantly used on such occasions. I mean, where people do penance for the great crimes of Adultery, Fornication, Perjury, or Incest. For lesser faults, I think, it may be omitted.

I make no doubt but so edifying a practice, so very agreeable to the way of the primitive Church, and so reasonable in itself, will be approved by you all, and conscientiously complied with.

I am,

Your affectionate friend and brother,

Thomas Sodor and Man.

¶ *When Penitents are to be received into the peace of the Church, you are to use the Form already in your hands; and at other times, this following Prayer only, with proper Exhortations.*

¶ *Let the Penitent be made sensible of the crimes for which he is censured; exhorted to humble himself before God and the Church; and especially to manifest the sincerity of his sorrow, by bringing forth fruits meet for repentance. After which all, kneeling, shall devoutly pray as followeth:*

¶ *THE PRAYER.*

O God, the Fountain of mercy, Who didst send Thy Son into the world to call sinners to repentance; and Who hath assured us, that there is joy in Heaven over one sinner that repenteth; look down with an eye of pity upon Thy servant, who has gone astray from Thy Commandments. Give *him* a clear sight of *his* sin, and a deep sense of Thy wrath against impenitent sinners; that seeing *his* danger, *he* may patiently submit to godly discipline, and to all the difficulties of true repentance. And grant, O God, that *he* may

not deceive *himself* by a counterfeit repentance; but that this public confession may
produce a real change of heart, and amendment of life; that *he* may utterly renounce
and forsake all evil ways; break off all evil
habits ; and being ever mindful of *his* infirmities, *he* may be more careful of *himself*, and
more earnest for grace for the time to come ;
working out *his* salvation with fear and
trembling ; that the Church on earth, and the
Angels in Heaven, may rejoice in *his* conversion.

Bless, O Lord, the discipline of this Church,
and make it effectual for the conviction of
wicked men and gainsayers. Vouchsafe unto
all penitents a true sense of their crimes, true
repentance for them, and Thy gracious pardon. Be merciful unto us all; and keep it
ever in the hearts of Thy servants, that it is
an evil thing and bitter to forsake the Lord.
Keep us from presumptuous sins; in all
temptations succour us, that no wickedness
may get the dominion over us ; but that continuing in the peace and unity of the Church

unto our lives' end, we may be made partakers of everlasting happiness with Thy Saints in Heaven, through Jesus Christ our Lord and Saviour. *Amen.*

¶ *Then shall the Minister say,*

May the gracious God give you repentance unto life eternal; receive you into His favour; continue you a true member of the Church of Christ; and bring you unto His everlasting Kingdom, through the same Jesus Christ our Lord. *Amen.*

————

At our Annual Convocation at Bishop's Court, Thursday in Whitsun Week, May 16, 1706.

THAT the Discipline of this Church may not degenerate or fall into contempt, it is thought meet by this Convocation, that the Form preceding be religiously observed (in the Mother Tongue) in all Churches and Chapels of this Diocese; and that none omit it under the severest Ecclesiastical censures.

That the Minister and Churchwardens, with some of the gravest of the Parishioners, shall, *bona fide*, certify unto the Bishop, that all this was performed after a decent and Christian manner; which Certificate, the person who has performed this censure shall be directed by his Pastor to bring himself within seven days, (and not to send it by any other person,) that he may receive the Bishop's blessing, and such spiritual counsel and advice as may tend to the good of his soul.

THOMAS SODOR AND MAN.
SAM. WATTLEWORTH, Archdeacon.
ROBERT PARR.
JO. CURGHEY.
THO. ALLEN.
JO. PARR.
HEN. NORRIS.
JO. COSNAHAN.
MATTH. CURGHEY.
J. WOODS.
EWAN GILL.
THO. CHRISTIAN.
WM. GELL.